JAH
IS OUR
GOD

DALTON "ELIJAH" GARRAWAY

This book is a work of non-fiction. Unless otherwise noted, the author and the publisher make no explicit guarantees as to the accuracy of the information contained in this book and in some cases, names of people and places have been altered to protect their privacy.

LifeRich Publishing is a registered trademark of The Reader's Digest Association, Inc.

LifeRich Publishing books may be ordered through booksellers or by contacting:

LifeRich Publishing
1663 Liberty Drive
Bloomington, IN 47403
www.liferichpublishing.com
844-686-9607

Because of the dynamic nature of the Internet, any web addresses or links contained in this book may have changed since publication and may no longer be valid. The views expressed in this work are solely those of the author and do not necessarily reflect the views of the publisher, and the publisher hereby disclaims any responsibility for them.

Any people depicted in stock imagery provided by Getty Images are models, and such images are being used for illustrative purposes only.
Certain stock imagery © Getty Images.

Scripture quotations taken from The Jerusalem Bible, copyright © 1966 by Darton, Longman & Todd, Ltd. and Doubleday, a division of Bantam Doubleday Dell Publishing Group, Inc. Reprinted by permission.

Scripture quotations marked KJV are from the Holy Bible, King James Version (Authorized Version). First published in 1611. Quoted from the KJV Classic Reference Bible, Copyright © 1983 by The Zondervan Corporation.

ISBN: 978-1-4897-3233-0 (sc)
ISBN: 978-1-4897-3234-7 (hc)
ISBN: 978-1-4897-3235-4 (e)

Library of Congress Control Number: 2020923673

Print information available on the last page.

LifeRich Publishing rev. date: 11/25/2020

Contents

Contents

Introduction

Hear, O Israel: The LORD our God is one LORD.
—Deuteronomy 6:4 (KJV)

THOSE WORDS OF the prophet Moses were spoken to the children of Israel some 1,430 years before the advent of the Messiah. He reassured them that their God was the one and only true God, and that they should have faith in him alone.

Every culture, every social group upon the face of our planet, shares some belief in the existence of a higher power, which we all (unawares) loosely call God. Religious scholars call that God consciousness.

Unfortunately, for some people in today's enlightened world, that higher power exists only in the form of idols fashioned in stone, wood, and precious metals. Others see that higher power in their money and earthly possessions. And even though the scripture says that "an idol is nothing in the world" (1 Corinthians 8:4 KJV), that is how some people conceive their god to be. And they seem to be more genuine than the few people who say there is no God at all. The scripture said that it's only "the fool who say in his heart that there is no God" (Psalm 14:1 KJV).

For though there be that are called gods (as there are gods many, and lords many), But to us there is

but one God, the Father who created all things. (1
Corinthians 8:5–6 KJV)

Now, who is this one God, the Father? How do we distinguish him
from those other gods? Does he have a name? And, if he does have a
personal name, what is it?

Unfortunately, in today's world of Christendom, the Father who
created all things has become known by one of two names, but neither
is his revealed, personal, proper name. Those two so-called names
have been exalted above other names and titles of honor, such as Lord,
Father, Creator, Almighty, and Highest.

Firstly, most people—Christians and non-Christians alike—
believe (probably due to ignorance) that God is the personal name
of our God, and they reiterate this by writing it with a capital G.
Notice that when we refer to many gods, we do not use an uppercase
G. Secondly, God has become known globally by the name Jehovah,
although in the original Hebrew and Greek scriptures, that name
was never mentioned!

Did our God refrain from mentioning his proper name when
he inspired the prophets of old to pen the Hebrew Bible—or did he
make it known, and evil men (in their efforts to deceive his children)
conspired to remove it from the scriptures?

Let it be known that our God intentionally mentioned his
personal name thousands of times in the Hebrew Bible. Thousands
of years ago, rabbinical scholars did, in fact, conspire to remove it
from the scriptures.

Obviously, because the name Jehovah was never mentioned in the
original Hebrew and Greek versions of the scriptures, it can never be
the revealed personal name of the Father who created all things. The
name Jehovah was fashioned simply by arbitrarily inserting the vowels
of the Hebrew word for *Lord* (in English) between the consonants of
the name our Creator had given himself. That was done with the sole
intent of concealing or blotting out the revealed personal name of our

God from the scriptures. Hence, most biblical scholars today agree that Jehovah is an artificially constructed name.

Moreover, our Creator has given himself a name that is much, much more than just a name. Let me explain by using Bob Marley's name as an example. I think it is fair for one to say that the late, great reggae king made a name for himself in the music industry. I also believe that all of us would agree that the name he made for himself was not Bob Marley. It was the reputation that he earned in the music industry. Although his personal name may have been Bob Marley, he became known as the king of reggae music.

Although Bob has passed on physically, his name still lives on among us. Therefore, if someone were to say that he or she was having a party and only music from the king of reggae would be played, no one would ask whose music would be playing. For want of an answer, however, one may reply, "Bob Marley's music," since the king of reggae has become synonymous with Bob Marley.

Are names important? And if names are truly important, what's really in a name?

In the biblical book of Exodus, Moses was inquiring about the personal name of our Father. Although all indications are that he had already known his name, God made it known to him. His reputation as the great, eternal I Am, the self-existent one, the immutable, omnipresent God was also made known to Moses on that occasion.

Addressing our Creator, Moses said,

> When I come unto the children of Israel, and shall say unto them, the God of your fathers hath sent me ... and they shall say unto me, What is his name? What shall I say unto them? (Exodus 3:13 KJV)

It is my belief that Moses truly wanted our God to verbally make his personal name known to him. He grew up in Egypt, where there were many gods, and all of them had personal names. In fact, even the political rulers, the pharaohs, had personal names and considered themselves to be gods.

Moses heard a voice speaking out of the burning bush, and he wanted to be sure that the voice was that of our Creator:

> I am the God of thy father, the God of Abraham ...
> Isaac ... and the God of Jacob. (Exodus 3:15 KJV)

In the original Hebrew text, the name our Creator revealed as his personal, proper name has only four letters, all of which are consonants. Accordingly, it became known as the four-letter name. In the English language, the letters are YHWH or JHWH/JHVH.

In the original version of the Jerusalem Bible, it is written:

> I AM He who is ... you are to tell the Israelites, YHWH, the God of your ancestors ... has sent me to you. This is my name for all times. (Exodus 3:14–15, Jerusalem Bible)

When I returned to the Brooklyn Central Library—where I did most of my early research—the original copy of the Jerusalem Version of the Bible that I had used was not available. The revised copy that was available had the four-letter name blotted out! Removing the four-letter name has now likened that trusted Jerusalem Version of the Bible to the King James Version.

As might be expected, the four-letter name, which is the proper name of our God, was replaced with the title *LORD* and the word *God*. And that tells me that even some modern biblical scholars suffer great discomfort when writing the name of God. They do not want us, the descendants of the children of Israel, to know our Father's name.

Nevertheless, in today's scriptures, anywhere you find the word *LORD* written in full capital letters, it tells us exactly where the proper name of our God was once written in the original ancient texts. This truth also applies to the word *God* if it is written in all uppercase letters. The title *Lord* first appeared in capital letters in Genesis 2:4 (KJV) of the scriptures. And interestingly, the fully capitalized word, Lord, appeared alongside the word, God, in that passage.

Therefore, when one reads the scriptures, one should, without any qualms, utter the sacred, revealed name instead of *Lord* or *God*, which our Father has given to himself.

Many centuries ago, during the period referred to as Second Temple Judaism (third to second centuries BCE) some misinformed rabbinical scholars—believing that the sacred, revealed name of God was too holy to be uttered by sinful man and afraid that the name would be taken in vain—took it upon themselves to substitute the Hebrew words *Adon* and *Adonai*, which mean *Lord* in English. In effect, they conspired and quite cunningly removed the personal name of our God from the scriptures!

Notwithstanding that, many reputable biblical scholars believe that YHWH may have been pronounced Yahweh or Yahawah with YAH as its shortened form.

Although there were no vowels in the ancient Hebrew alphabet, the English vowels "a" and "e" were conveniently added to the four consonants to aid in vocalization. However, the makers of the *Expository Dictionary of Bible Words* imply that pronouncing the four-letter name as Yahweh amounts to a scholarly guess of what the name would have sounded like when vocalized.

Further, many scholars agree that when anglicized, the name can be pronounced Jahweh. Jah is its constricted or shortened form. *The Harper Collins Bible Dictionary* clearly states that Jahweh/Jah is a substitute transcription of Yahweh.

It is my belief that the rabbinical scholars, despite their uncertainty, never promoted Jahweh/Jah as an equal pronunciation of the four-letter name—probably because they spoke the Hebrew language, and in the Hebrew alphabet, there is no letter *J*. I believe they were either ignorant of or were—quite dishonestly—willing to ignore the fact that there are similarities in the sounds produced by different letters in any alphabet, in any language during vocalization.

Language experts said, for instance, that in the German alphabet, the letter *J* is pronounced like the letter *Y* in English. And that also holds true for the same letter *Y* in the Hebrew alphabet and the letter *J* in English. In the English alphabet, there are vowels and a letter *J*. Therefore, this writer—as a Rasta man who happens to have an English tongue—does promote Jahweh/Jah as the preferred pronunciation of the sacred name:

> I am Jahweh/Jah. To Abraham, Isaac, and Jacob, I appeared as El Shaddai [Almighty God] But I did not make my name, Jahweh/Jah, known to them. (Exodus 6:2–3 Jerusalem Bible)

> The Lord [Jah] is not slack concerning his promise, as some men count slackness. (2 Peter 3:9 KJV).

> Let it be known that every word which comes out of the mouth of the living God, Jah, is true, and shall be established. It was the prophet, Habakkuk, whose name literally means, embrace, take up and cherish, who said, "At the end it shall speak, and not lie; though it tarries, wait for it, because it will surely come." (Habakkuk 2:3 KJV)

Now, in the seventh chapter of the second book of Samuel, our Creator told David, king of Israel, that after he (David) would have gone the way of the world or departed this earth, one of his descendants would be chosen to build a house for his name. Here, *house* does not simply mean residence or place of abode; it is also a people who would bear and proclaim the name of their God and fill the earth with the knowledge of his glory.

Further, the Lord promised David that he would establish his house and his kingdom forever:

> And thine house and thy kingdom shall be established forever before thee; thy throne shall be established forever. (2 Samuel 7:16 KJV)

Remember, that the Lord had given him the house of Israel and of Judah (2 Samuel 12:8 KJV).

As might be expected, David passed then "sat Solomon upon the throne of David, his father" (1 Kings 2:12 KJV).

As tradition would have had it, Adonijah, Solomon's older brother, thought he should have succeeded David, but the Lord chose Solomon instead to be ruler over Israel and over Judah. In support of this, King David, while addressing the host of Israel said, "Of all my sons, the Lord hath chosen Solomon to sit upon the throne of the kingdom of the LORD over Israel" (1 Chronicles 28:5 KJV).

The title *LORD*, in the quotation above, is written in uppercase letters. That meant that when King David addressed the host of Israel on that historic occasion, he deliberately chose to utter the sacred name of his God, our God, Jah. Again, wherever the title *Lord* appears in the scriptures with all the letters fully capitalized, it tells us exactly where the sacred name, Jah, was once written in the original Hebrew text.

It is my belief that, at some point, Adonijah thought that their father, David, would die before Solomon was anointed king. If that happened, then he would become king instead of his younger brother. Solomon would then be "counted as an offender" (1 Kings 1:21 KJV) and could be put to death.

The future of the throne of the Davidic kingdom depended on Solomon and not on Adonijah or on any other son of David. It was Jah—and not King David—who chose Solomon to sit upon the throne "of the kingdom of the LORD [Jah] over Israel" (1 Chronicles 28:5 KJV).

David's public proclamation gave great displeasure to Adonijah. Therefore, believing that the ailing king's words would soon become invalid, he ordered a priest, Abiathar—who was later removed from the priesthood—to anoint him king instead of his brother, Solomon.

After his self-proclaimed kingship became public, the aging King David—fearing that the one whom the Lord had chosen to sit upon the throne of the kingdom of the Lord over Israel might not be regarded as the rightful king—immediately ordered Zadok, the priest, and Nathan, the prophet, to anoint Solomon as king.

Then, fearing for his own life, Adonijah asked for Solomon's forgiveness. Nevertheless, he was still dissatisfied and complained to Bathsheba, Solomon's mother:

> Thou knowest that the kingdom was mine, and that all Israel set their faces on me, that I should reign; howbeit, the kingdom is turned about, and is become my brother's; for it was his from the LORD [Jah]. (1 Kings 2:15 KJV)

Adonijah knew Jah had chosen Solomon to sit upon the throne.

Immediately after the death of David, Adonijah—still unhappy that his brother was anointed king—expressed more displeasure by demanding that Solomon gave him Abishag in marriage. He conveniently chose Solomon's mother as his messenger because he taught that the king would not deny her request. Abishag was the fair, young Shunammite virgin who cherished, and ministered to King David during his last days.

Even though David never had a sexual encounter with her, her service to the ailing king was such as would be expected of one's wife:

> King David was old and stricken in years; and they covered him with clothes, but he got no heat. (1 Kings 1:1 KJV)

The king had literally become so old and cold that not even several layers of clothing could make him warm. Abishag was brought into his court to make the king warm.

Remember, the king was very old and no doubt would have lost his sexual appetite as it were. Therefore, he had no need for another virgin wife. The only known cure for the ailing king's condition was some "contactual medicine."

During those days (about 971 BC), many God-fearing people believed that body heat had therapeutic properties and that body heat was transferrable from a young virgin's body to an older ailing body. Therefore, David would let Abishag "lie in his bosom, so that he may get heat" (1 Kings 1:2 KJV).

The makers of the *Anchor Bible Dictionary* (vol. 1) confirmed that contactual medicine was a common practice in ancient times. Also, they acknowledged that the renowned Jewish historian Josephus attested to that ancient practice.

I think it expedient here to quickly say a little more about Josephus. I am not at all happy to mention him only by name. He was a first-century Jewish historian, soldier, and political activist. In his second piece of writing, known as the *Jewish Antiquities*, he unearthed the history of the Hebrew people from the earliest times to the Jewish war of 66–70 CE. He received much of his knowledge by observing the three sects of Jewry known during his day: the Sadducees, the Pharisees, and the Essenes. Although he was a self-proclaimed Pharisee from the age of nineteen, he was essentially the scribe of his time.

Even though the word *Semitic* relates more to language than to ethnicity, the early sects of Judaism were of so-called Semitic origin. Unlike almost all of modern Jewry, they were of the seed of Abraham, Isaac, and Jacob.

One must never forget that Jah changed Jacob's name to Israel, and then he became the father of the people of Israel. Israel, therefore, is a people and not a landmass. That means that they were all Hebrew-Israelites.

Outside of the scriptures, Josephus has proven himself most useful as a source for the history of Christianity and Judaism. During the Middle Ages, many looked up to him as though he was a church father. His writings have also been dubbed a "Fifth Gospel" as well as the "Small Bible." And to this day, that is the reason most reputable Bible scholars and historians in general rely so heavily on his writings.

The *Harper Collins Bible Dictionary* confirms that when one mentions the term Hebrew, they are referring to the people of Israel, the descendants of Abraham. The Bible said that Abraham was called a Hebrew long before the term *Jew* had been penned. In fact, that is the first time we encounter the word *Hebrew* in the Bible (Genesis 14:13 KJV).

According to Genesis 11:28, 31 (KJV), Abram/Abraham came from the city of Ur of the Chaldees. Archaeological records show that Ur was located in southern Mesopotamia as we know it today.

Godfrey Higgins (1772–1833), a renowned, honest religious historian and antiquarian of English stock declared, "The Chaldees were originally Negroes" (*Anacalypsis*, volume 2, 364). Clearly, Mr. Higgins had no qualms about writing the truth. He knew that the truth cannot be hidden forever.

All the descendants of Abraham knew themselves as Hebrew and nothing else. Even our disobedient prophet, Jonah, was proud of that. Just before they tossed him overboard, the shipmaster asked, "And of what people are you?' Jonah replied with a boast: "I am Hebrew" (Jonah 1:8–9 KJV).

Paul, the questionable, shady, Roman soldier of the New Testament, loved referring to himself as "a Hebrew of the Hebrews" (Philippians 3:5 KJV).

The term *Jew* was used loosely to refer to those people who were expelled from Judah during the time when Pekah—the wayward king who ruled Israel from 740–732 BC—conspired with Rezin, the king of Syria, and invaded Judah (2 Kings 16:5–6 KJV). Some of the people who inhabited Judah were also called men of Judah, Judahites, or Judeans.

While reading a piece about Josephus in *The Anchor Bible Dictionary*, I found out that his writings caused great discomfort among many of his Jewish counterparts who were living in Jerusalem during his time. And even today, in the world of modern Jewry, some Jewish scholars still underrate his writings. He loved talking and writing about what transpired during the time between the Testaments. He also wrote a lot about John the Baptist and declared that Eyesus Kristos (Jesus Christ) was a real historical figure and a simple, dark-skinned man.

By dwelling among some sects of modern Jewry, I have come to realize that they do not think so favorably of Eyesus. Some scholars say that it's because he was born in a manger, did not come in pomp and glory, and did not appear as the long-awaited political messiah who would outlaw the Roman political system and institute his own. There is, however, an admirable growing movement among modern Jewry called Jews for Jesus.

Josephus wrote that "there lived (during the time when Pontius Pilate was governor of Judaea) Jesus [Eyesus] a wise man, if indeed one ought to call him a man" (*Anchor Bible Dictionary*, 990). Clearly, to him, Eyesus was more than man.

Historical records prove that Pontius Pilate was the fifth governor of the Roman province. He served from around 26/27 to 36/37 CE. He presided over the trial of Jesus and had him put to death.

In *The Thirteenth Tribe*, Arthur Koestler, a Jewish author, questioned the ancestry of modern-world Jewry and concluded that they are probably not of Abraham's seed at all. Available historical records show that they came mostly from the Eastern European Khazar Empire. Their leaders converted to the Jewish faith around AD 740 and declared Judaism their state religion. Unless one's ancestry is rooted in that of Abraham, the Hebrew, one cannot truly consider himself or herself to be a Hebrew or Israelite. In effect, one does not become a Hebrew-Israelite by conversion.

Now let us return to Abishag. Although the aging king never had a sexual encounter with her, she still became part of his harem. In fact, the most sacred Ethiopian text, the *Kebra Nagast* (translated by E. A. Wallis Budge), referred to her as "the wife of his father David." After David passed, she remained in Solomon's court. Adonijah's request to have her in marriage displeased Solomon, and he regarded her highly for the service she offered to their father and could not allow Adonijah to defile her.

Abishag's presence in Solomon's court was of political significance; therefore, there was no way he was going to let his brother have her in marriage. Solomon thought he had inherited the throne—and Abishag. She was like a gift, a token of his kingship, from his father. Remember, David did not know her, and as far as he was concerned, his brother's request to have her in marriage amounted to an attempt to usurp the throne.

Accordingly, Solomon's reply to his mother was this: "Ask for him the kingdom also" (1 Kings 2:19–22 KJV).This time, in the king's mind, his brother was guilty of treason; therefore, he ordered that he be put to death.

Adonijah showed disrespect and complained about Solomon's ascent to the throne of their father, David, and he also challenged the power and authority of Jah. Jah had overlooked the traditions of men and chose Solomon to sit upon the throne. The traditions of men are not always in keeping with the decrees of our Father, Jah.

Solomon reigned, and his kingdom was established greatly:

> And there came from all peoples to hear the wisdom
> of Solomon, from all Kings of the earth, who had
> heard of his wisdom. (1 Kings 4:34 KJV)

Among those who visited Solomon was the famous "Queen of the South," better known in the Bible as the queen of Sheba. And our sacred Ethiopian text, the *Kebra Nagast*, affirmed that the Queen of the South was the queen of Ethiopia, and her proper name was Makeda.

What was so important about Queen Makeda that she found her way into the Bible? Why, out of all the kings and queens who visited

Solomon, the scriptures seem to have her in such high esteem? Even Eyesus made mention of her one day:

> The queen of the south shall rise up in the judgement with this generation, and shall condemn it; for she came from the uttermost parts of the earth to hear the wisdom of Solomon. (Matthew 12:42 KJV)

One can imagine what she endured on that perilous journey to Jerusalem. According to the *Kebra Nagast*, "she thought it was too far and too difficult to undertake" (21). Also, she abandoned sun worship to serve Jah, our God whom Solomon served. Further, she was the one chosen to bring forth that promised seed of David through the lineage of King Solomon. Our Ethiopian text says that it was all the good pleasure and the will of our God, Jah (21).

Although most scholars hold that Sheba was located in the southwestern part of Arabia, it was part of Ethiopia. When the Bible spoke about Ethiopia, it meant far more than the country, Ethiopia, in northeast Africa, which we all know today. In *The Real Facts About Ethiopia*, J. A. Rogers agreed with the renowned father of history, Herodotus (525–484 BC) who held that, at one time, Ethiopia's boundaries included Egypt and the rest of the continent of Africa, all of Arabia, and parts of Southeast Asia, extending into western India.

The *Harper Collins Bible Dictionary* mentioned that even Homer—in the sixth century BCE—mentioned that Ethiopia's boundary extended into Saudi Arabia and Yemen (*Odyssey*, 1.22–23). All of Palestine and the well-sought-after and war-fought-over land of Israel are part and parcel of Ethiopia, the Holy Land.

The actual word *Ethiopia* means burnt faces or dark skin. In addition, pages 16, 53, and 163 of *The Kebra Nagast* (the version translated by E. A. Wallis Budge) give similar details regarding Ethiopia's earliest biblical boundary markings. In ancient times, all the people living within those landmarks were black, and they all had dark skin or burnt faces.

The scriptures mention Sheba's visit"

> She came to Jerusalem … she talked with Solomon
> about all that was in her heart … and the King gave
> unto her all her desire … she gave the king gold,
> spices and precious stones … she turned and went to
> her own country. (1 Kings 10:1–13 KJV)

Interestingly, the scripture said that what compelled Queen Makeda to go up to Jerusalem was not so much Solomon's wisdom or because he was widely acclaimed and honored; it was "his fame concerning the name of the LORD [Jah]" (1 Kings 10:1 KJV).

We know from the *Kebra Nagast* that the queen of Ethiopia heard about Solomon through one of her servants and merchants: "She asked Tamrin questions about Solomon … and he told her about him" (21). After Solomon started building the House for Jah, he wanted specific building materials. He invited merchants from all countries, near and far, to bring what their country had in exchange for gold, oil, and food. One trader told Solomon about a wealthy Ethiopian merchant named Tamrin.

When Solomon contacted Tamrin, a wise man, he asked him to bring certain items that he knew were easily accessible along his trade route. Those building materials include sapphires, red gold, and black wood, which was resistant to termites. Tamrin conducted business by sea and by land. He commanded a fleet of seventy-three ships and had about 520 camels, all of which belonged to the queen of Ethiopia.

While conducting business in the Holy Land, Tamrin observed the king, and he was astonished by the way he commanded the respect and cooperation of his subjects. Upon his return to Ethiopia, he told the queen everything he had seen and heard from Solomon. The queen of Sheba must have heard that Solomon praised the name of Jah and that he declared that his God was Jah and that he has been exalted above all other so-called gods. Also, she must have heard that Jah, Solomon's God, was the Creator of the heavens and the earth.

She had also heard that his God came down and spoke to him. In addition, she must have heard that Solomon's God had chosen him to build a house for him to dwell in, a settled place for him to abide in forever.

The queen of Sheba felt that if the God who created the heavens and the earth would choose a human being to build a house for him to abide in forever, then that person must be a very special person. Therefore, as stated in the *Kebra Nagast*, she became "exceedingly anxious to go to him," and "see his face, and embrace him" (21).

While in Jerusalem, the queen of Sheba confessed to Solomon that she was a sun worshipper and that she believed the sun was the king of the gods. Nevertheless, she was convinced that Solomon's God—whom she did not yet know—was the true and living God since he sometimes came down and talked with Solomon. As might be expected, she asked Solomon who was the right God for her to worship.

After she found out that Solomon's God made the sun, which she worshipped, she was astonished. She figured out that the maker of the sun was higher than the sun itself. She made up her mind to never worship the sun again. She decided to worship Jah, the God of Israel, the Creator of the sun.

Before she left to return to her country, "there was no more spirit in her" (1 Kings 10:5 KJV) She remarked, "Thy wisdom and prosperity exceeds the fame which I heard" (1 Kings 10:7 KJV).

The queen fell in love with the king, and she overstayed her time in Jerusalem. In fact, Tamrin warned her that anyone who was fortunate enough to observe King Solomon did not wish to leave him and go away from him, and she proved that to be true. In fact, our Ethiopian text said that soon after she met the king, she began to experience such great feelings of awe that she could not resist telling him how "she wished she was one of his female servants, so that she

In the book of Kings, we learn that Solomon loved many strange women. In our Ethiopian text, he described the queen of Ethiopia as a woman of "splendid beauty" (*Kebra Nagast*, 30). And to him, a woman who possessed such beauty was worth having. Therefore, as he reasoned with her daily, he became convinced that the Lord probably brought her to him so that he could have "seed in her" (*Kebra Nagast*, 30). She spent six months in Jerusalem as his very special guest, and there is no doubt in my mind that the king would have done whatever it took to sleep with her. In fact, our Ethiopian text details exactly how and what he did to get her in bed (34–35).

It is rather unfortunate that the scribes of the modern Bible failed to mention that King Solomon and the queen had an intimate sexual affair, which resulted in the birth of a male child known as Bayna Lehkem. That name literally means son of the wise man. There is no doubt the sages who were involved in the canonizing of the scripture—as we know it today—also knew that to be a true because it has been documented, and they were in possession of such writings.

Gerald Hausman's version of the *Kebra Nagast* (the version with an introduction by Ziggy Marley, son of Bob Marley) mentioned that King James's fifty-four scholars had a copy of it in their possession when they were putting the 1611 KJV of the scriptures together. Unfortunately, like many other sacred writings, it was conveniently left out of the KJV Bible. Maybe it was too Ethiopic—too black—for King James and his learned scholars.

When Bayna was a young man, he visited his father, Solomon, in Jerusalem. He wore the signet ring that his father had given to his mother. Solomon knew that when the youth became an adult, he would want to know his father; therefore, he instructed her to let him wear it when he went to Jerusalem.

The people in Jerusalem saw him as the spitting image of his father. Everyone knew he was the king's son, whom he begot with Makeda.

As the Lord, Jah, would have it, upon his return to Ethiopia, he took with him the Ark of the Covenant, which they called the "heavenly Zion." The same day it arrived in Ethiopia, it gave off rays of light just like the sun.

The Ark of the Covenant was sent to Ethiopia because Solomon, by that time, had begun to corrupt himself:

> His wives turned away his heart after other gods. (1 Kings 11:4 KJV)

> The LORD was angry with Solomon, because his heart was turned from the LORD. (1 Kings 11:9 KJV)

The presence of the Ark of the Covenant in the center of Ethiopia signified the establishment of the new Jerusalem as well as the Davidic lineage of kings in that country. Makeda abdicated the throne around 955 BC, and Bayna became emperor of Ethiopia. He was called King David, but he later adopted the throne name Menelik I, which also means son of the wise man.

In passing, Bayna got the name David after Zadok, the priest in Jerusalem, anointed him king of Ethiopia, when he visited Solomon. Even before his mother abdicated, he had already been proclaimed king of Ethiopia.

The Most High, in accordance with his covenant, announced through Jeremiah, the prophet, that the days shall surely come when he "will raise unto David a righteous Branch, and a King shall reign and prosper, and shall execute judgment and justice in the earth" (Jeremiah 23:5 KJV).

> A root of Jessie ... shall rise ... again the second time ... to recover his people. (Isaiah 11:1, 10–11 KJV)

The righteous root of Jessie must come out of Ethiopia, and that king (earth's rightful ruler) must be a direct descendant of King Solomon and the queen of Ethiopia. And we found that king in none other than Emperor Haile Selassie I, who traced his lineage forward to our king and queen.

Even if we, the children of the Most High, were to wait until the end of time comes, the Vatican will never acknowledge that truth because they still believe what we, the Hebrew- Israelites, cannot know anything except what they tell us. Let it be known that what has been hidden from the wise and prudent has been revealed to babes and suckling.

Haile Selassie literally means power/might of the Holy Trinity! That is how we know Haile Selassie is the promised righteous branch of David, according to the flesh. Through that wonderful name, he declared to the world that he was part of the Godhead.

Emperor Haile Selassie was the returned Messiah, and Jah raised him up for the second time to redeem his people. Eyesus Kristos, the Hebrew-Israelite Christ, made his Second Coming in the personality of Haile Selassie I of Ethiopia. I was awestruck when I found out that J. A. Rogers, a renowned author, advocated that Haile Selassie was a black edition of the pictured Christ.

No one can deny that today's pictured Christ is a not a black one. The pictured Christ on the calendar is the one every householder was once upon a time proud to hang upon the walls of their living rooms, bedrooms, kitchens, and bathrooms.

In 1505, Pope Julius II ordered Michelangelo to paint certain biblical characters. As might be expected, he painted them all like himself (Caucasian).

It is a historical fact that the earliest paintings of Mary and her son depicted them as black; unfortunately, during the Renaissance, their images were deliberately altered to look like a white woman and son. They left no trace of their original blackness.

When Haile Selassie taught humanity how to live, the League of Nations—the predecessor of today's United Nations—put him to the test. He passed through the fire, and he came out as pure gold. After the Vatican realized who Haile Selassie truly was, Pope Pious XI commissioned a crusade against him. His Majesty prevailed, proving himself worthy of being called the Conquering Lion of the Tribe of Judah.

Today, the people who choose to walk the way of life known as Rastafari—not Rastafarianism because Rastas do not dwell with isms and schisms—stands firm upon this tenet. Many people who wear the crown of life, dreadlocks, are still not aware of that basic tenet of Rastafari. Wearing the crown is evidence that one has embarked on that spiritual journey.

Only the Rasta man wears the crown of life. It represents the consecration of our God, Jah, which is upon his head. His locks are the outward, visible sign that he has separated himself unto—and is willing to bear reproach for—the name of Jah.

The apostle Paul's opinion on this particular issue is in direct conflict with what Moses taught our ancestors. And, in this time, the Rasta man has chosen to obey Moses rather than Paul. Paul wrote, "If a man has long hair, it is a shame unto him" (1 Corinthians 11:14 KJV). He seemed more inclined to follow the traditions of men rather than the words our God, Jah, gave to Moses. He must have known better than to make such a misleading statement. Every Nazarite—every man or woman, past or present—who seeks to walk with the Lord, was commanded to "let the locks of the hair of his or her hair grow" (Numbers 6:5 KJV):

> When either man or woman shall separate themselves to vow a vow of a Nazarite, to separate themselves unto Jah ... All the days of the vow of his separation there shall no razor come upon his head ... he shall be holy and shall let the locks of the hair of his head grow. (Numbers 6:2–5 KJV)

The imitation locks a hairdresser gives to a bald head man are not dreadlocks; they are "dead locks." After an hour or two in the hair salon, he can emerge with dead locks cascading down his torso. The accuser of the brethren likes to imitate; instead of carrying the consecration of Jah, he chose to carry dead locks upon his head, and that ought to be a shame to him.

As far as salvation is concerned, our God, Jah, has already saved us, the descendants of the children of Israel, whom Moses brought out of Egyptian slavery. As his prized creation, he has saved us from sin or what learned clergymen like to call *original sin*. By now, most of us know how they loved to drive home the lie that we were all born in sin.

Let it be known that in the same way that our first parents (Adam and Eve) brought original sin upon humanity, so did Eyesus Kristos (Jesus the Christ), through the spiritual genetic engineering feat he wrought on the cross, has freed us from the penalties of original sin. And that is something we could not have done for ourselves. Therefore, we need not worry ourselves anymore about the consequences of sin.

Nobody born after Eyesus (Jesus) died on the cross was born in sin. Caiaphas, the high priest at the temple in Jerusalem when Eyesus was crucified, boldly spoke to the learned chief priests and Pharisees:

> You know nothing at all … that it is expedient for us that one man should die for the people. (John 11:49–50 KJV)

I believe him because it is written that what he said was actually inspired by the spirit of the Most High. He actually prophesied about the death of Eyesus (see John 11:51 KJV).

Have you ever wondered why, after thousands of years in the world of Christendom, we are being constantly told that we need to be saved? And, by the way, if we still need to be saved, what do we have to be saved from?

Christians have not yet been able to grasp exactly what Eyesus did on the cross. They preach and teach that to be saved, we must be washed in the blood. Black men, in particular, must become as white as snow. That is foolishness. They also teach that humans will eventually be saved when we reach "over yonder." Therefore, many of us believe in them, but that is religious bigotry.

They see salvation as an otherworldly issue: a pie in the sky. The only salvation we, the people who are called by the name of Jah, our God, hope for is physical, earthly salvation. God shall save us from our present-day Egyptians, our present-day oppressors:

> I will gather the remnant of my flock out of all countries to which I have driven them and will bring them again to their folds; and they shall be fruitful and increase. (Jeremiah 23:3 KJV)

Our God, Jah, warned the black Hebrew-Israelites who came out of Egypt with Moses about what would happen if they did not do what he required them to do:

> Scatter them among all people, from the one end of the earth even unto the other ... and shall bring them into Egypt [bondage], again with ships ... and they shall be sold unto their enemies for male and female slaves, and no man shall buy them. (Deuteronomy 28:64, 68 KJV)

When the scripture said that "no man shall buy them," it means that no one will be truly interested in our redemption. Had it not been for the goodness of our God, Jah, slavery would still be legal today. When it was said that our ancestors were freed from slavery in this part of the world, that was neither freedom nor redemption. Freedom during those days meant nothing more than to be free and dumb. The Rasta man embraces redemption—and not that ignoble brand of freedom.

The dispersion referred to in the above scripture intensified around AD 70 when the Romans overran the Holy Land. It was completed during the transatlantic slave trade, which lasted (legally) for more than three hundred years. Throughout those years, tens of millions of black Hebrew-Israelites who dwelled in the kingdom of Judah in Negro Land, Africa, were taken across the Atlantic Ocean and sold as slaves.

There is good news, however. Our wasted years of captivity in the so-called New World will soon be over, and then—and only then— we shall know what it truly means to be saved. That is the salvation that we, the descendants of those who survived the African Holocaust, hope for in this time.

The scriptures are essentially centered on the people of the Most High: those who are called by his name. At this time, only one set of people is called by his name: Rastafari. These people see Haile Selassie as Jah-Rastafari, and they are the only people on this earth who, like Elijah, the prophet, declare that their God is Jah.

Our God has raised us (Rastas) up to declare his name to the world in these last days. We are a sign of the time. We were born Rasta; we did not become or turn Rasta as some people like to put it. Some of us took longer than others to grow up and put on the crown. What we purpose to do in this time is to humble ourselves, pray, seek Jah's face, and turn from Babylon and their wicked and deceitful ways. God will hear us, and he will forgive our trespasses, and we shall, again, become fruitful and increase.

Moreover, our God said, all that we need to do in this time is to "return unto him, for he has already redeemed us" (Isaiah 44:22 KJV). Jah is the one who has bought us with a price that no man on this earth could have paid.

Yes, our God, Jah, shall see to it, and we shall return to Ethiopia, the biblical Ethiopia, with its biblical boundaries restored. He is the one who established the boundaries within which all nations shall dwell. We shall dwell within the boundaries he has assigned to us—and not within those that our enemies and oppressors have confined us to.

It is written that the day is coming when we shall say:

The LORD [Jah] liveth, who brought up and who
led the seed of the house of Israel out of the north
country, and from all countries to which I had
driven them, and they shall dwell in their own land.
(Jeremiah 23:8 KJV)

Jah said so, and so shall it be when the fullness of time comes.

This book aims to provide some spiritual nourishment so the
disciples of Rastafari can always be ready to give an answer to anyone
who wants to know the reason we hope in Haile Selassie I: the power/
might of the Holy Trinity, Root of David, according to the flesh.

The Highest God, Jah, shall bless and keep whosoever shall read
the pages of this book with an open mind. Selah.

Chapter 1

The Sacred Name: Jah

LUCKILY, WHAT HAPPENED to our first parents in Eden did not deprive humanity of God consciousness. Hence, every culture upon the face of our planet possesses some knowledge of the existence of a higher power or Supreme Being.

Unfortunately, this Supreme Being, for some people, took the form of idols carved in wood, stone, or precious metals. For others, he was the moon, the sun, or even groups of stars that form patterns in the sky.

Outside of Eden, the need for a god was so pressing that humanity created its own gods. It is written that "every nation made gods of their own" (2 Kings 17:29 KJV).

Interestingly, it has been documented in the *Kebra Nagast* that when Abram (whose name was later changed to Abraham) was a young man, he helped his father (who was an idol maker) market idol gods. Apparently, that was his family's main source of income. When Abram realized that the idols he sold were gods that could not make deliverance, he mocked them and tossed them to the ground. He called upon the Creator of the heavens and the earth, admonishing him to be his God (*Kebra Nagast*, 9–10).

Notwithstanding that, I believe that some people genuinely thought they could connect with the Supreme Being by having a visible, tangible god at their disposal. Not that they believed their

1

carved image was that higher power, but it was a representation of that higher power—something that would constantly remind them of his existence and his omnipresence.

On the other hand, I also believe that one can easily fall into idolatry without even realizing it. Let me explain. A few days after Moses's seeming disappearance on Mount Sinai, the children of Israel, having recognized their need for God, said to Aaron, "Make us gods, which shall go before us" (Exodus 32:1 KJV). They no doubt thought that Moses had deserted them; he was gone forever and, apparently, had taken the God of Israel with him:

> "As for this Moses who brought us out of the land of Egypt," they mocked, "we do not know what is become of him." (Exodus 32:1 KJV)

As far as they were concerned, the only solution was for them to make their own gods; therefore, Aaron made the golden calf:

> These are thy gods, O Israel ... and they ... offered burnt offering. (Exodus 32:4–6 KJV)

Can you imagine Aaron, the Levite, the very first high priest, of all the elders of Israel, who experienced the powers of the great I Am daily, now offering burnt offerings to a golden calf? Did he really believe the idol was a god that could replace the great I Am? The answer is no. I believe that Aaron acted out of sympathy for the people. He thought that if he could give them something tangible they could call god until Moses's return (with the true God), then it may give them some sense of spiritual well-being.

Despite his engineering of the golden calf, Aaron continued in his high priestly office until his death. Our God, Jah, looked beyond Aaron's idolatry. And like his brother, Moses, he never entered the Promised Land.

Why did the Lord himself, the one who commanded his people

not to make carved images, later order Moses—the one who taught his commands—to make the serpent of bronze to save them from snakebites? (Numbers 21:8 KJV).

That bronze serpent became an object of idolatrous worship for hundreds of years after the passing of Moses. It was destroyed only after Hezekiah (716–687 BC) became king of Judah. He was the thirteenth king of Judah after the death of King Solomon:

> He [Hezekiah] … broke in pieces the bronze serpent
> that Moses had made. (2 Kings 18:4 KJV)

It is evident from the scriptures that some nations were so committed to their idol gods that they even had a dedicated priesthood who would bestow names upon and minister daily to those so-called gods.

During the time of the prophet Daniel, for example, the Babylonians worshipped an idol god named Bel. On page 111 of the authorized King James version of *The Apocrypha* (as it relates to the story of Bel and the dragon), the Babylonian priests would lavish Bel with "twelve full measures of refined flour, forty sheep, and six large containers of fine wine" daily.

Even though the king (Cyrus of Persia) thought that extravagant, he conceded because he truly believed that his god, Bel, was consuming the offering. On that very occasion when Daniel visited with the king, he boastingly asked Daniel if he was not at all impressed by the amount of food and drink that the idol god was supposedly consuming on a daily basis? (Bel and the Dragon, 111, verse 6, *The Apocrypha*). There is, therefore, no doubt that the king believed that Bel was a living god. As a result, he would go to the temple daily to adore it and worship it. He even suggested that Daniel do the same (Bel and the Dragon, 111, verse 4, *The Apocrypha*).

As might be expected, Daniel refused:

> I am not supposed to worship idols made with
> hands, but the living God, who created the heaven

> and the earth. (Bel and the Dragon, 111, verse 5,
> *The Apocrypha*)

After a brief chiding by Daniel, the king was filled with wrath and ordered his priests to prove that Bel was truly eating the daily offering. Otherwise, they would be put to death.

When Daniel and the king returned to the temple the next morning, the offering was gone. Thankfully, the ashes that Daniel had sprinkled on the floor of the temple the night before in the presence of the king revealed that the priests and their families had entered the temple at night through a secret passage and consumed the offering made to Bel.

Had Daniel not exposed the trickery of the priests, the king and the entire nation would no doubt have continued to believe that Bel was a living god. The king realized that the priests had been practicing deceit ever since Bel was erected, and he ordered that the entire priesthood and their families be put to death.

The king gave Daniel the authority to destroy the idol gods (both Bel and the dragon). As might be expected, the king abandoned idol worship.

Even though humanity, at some point in time, did worship idols in its quest to reunite with its Creator, they knew that the idol was not the Living God. That was humanity's feeble attempt to regain its godlikeness. Therefore, they made idols and worshipped them, knowing that the Living God created them (human beings) and that they were created to worship the Living God.

Today, in our efforts to set the true and Living God apart and "above all that is also called god, or that is worshipped (for there are many gods and many lords)" (1 Corinthians 8:5 KJV), we think it expedient to bestow countless names and titles of honor upon the one true God of creation. We often address him as the Father, the Almighty, the Most High, the Lord, the Eternal One, Jehovah, and in fact, simply as God, written with a capital "G." One Christian sect even advocates that we hyphenate, and write G-d instead of God.

I was told that writing G-d instead of God is honorable because when God is spelled backward, the word dog appears, and one must not, in any way, associate God with dogs. That is ridiculous!

It should be noted, nonetheless, that all those titles and names of honor that we have employed to distinguish the one true God from all that is also called god, are not, in themselves, names per se. They were penned over centuries as humanity learned about the attributes and personal character of the one true God. He is given a name when he provides material things for his people and when he makes them triumph over an enemy in battle and the like.

Name, in this sense, does not necessarily mean a personal name, but rather a phrase or word that expresses what the God of creation proved himself to be in any given situation. In other words, when his people realized he could meet all their needs, they gave him a name that reflected what he had done. When, for example, he provided material things for them, they attached the title JIREH to his name, and when he made them triumph over an enemy in battle, they aptly used the term NISSI.

Since Abraham knew God by the name, El Shaddai (Almighty), he gave the name El Shaddai-JIREH to the place where he offered the ram for a burnt offering in the stead of his son Isaac. El Shaddai-JIREH means the Almighty will provide. The Almighty now became known as the Almighty Provider.

In most versions of the Bible, the place where the burnt offering was made is wrongly called Jehovah-JIREH because Jehovah is not the proper name of God (see Genesis 22:14 KJV). In fact, the name Jehovah was not known to humanity during those days. Likewise, Moses gave the name YHWH-NISSI to the altar he erected to honor the Lord after his victory over Amalek. YHWH-NISSI means the Lord is my banner or take hold of the banner of YHWH. Some transliterations of Exodus 17:15 (KJV), call the altar Jehovah-NISSI. Again, that is wrong because Jehovah is not the proper name of our Lord.

Moses employed the Hebrew noun *Elohim* when he wrote the Creation story (Genesis 1:1 KJV). Elohim was the prevalent word

5

used during that time to denote deity. That noun is translated as God in English. El is the singular form of the noun; hence, the one who created the heavens and the earth was rightfully and most aptly called the Creator. However, Creator, we would all concede, is not the name of the God of creation.

In effect, calling God God is like calling the leader of a republic Mr. President. Although the leader is indeed the president, he does have a personal name, and that name should be used to distinguish him from all past and future presidents.

It is noteworthy that Eyesus Kristos (Jesus Christ), did use that same noun, El, while he was nailed to the cross. No doubt, one would remember when he cried out, "Eli, Eli, La Ma sabachthani? My God, my God, why hast thou forsaken me?" (Matthew 27:46 KJV). El, as we know, is an ancient Hebrew word for God, "i" is the subject pronoun, and "my" is the possessive determiner.

When the people who were present at the crucifixion heard him said, "Eli, Eli," they thought he was calling for the prophet, Elijah, to help him. They all knew that the very name of the God who Elijah served was enshrined in the very name of Elijah!

In Genesis 14:18 (KJV), Moses employed another Hebrew word, *El Elyon*, which, in English, literally means highest. The Highest God, the one who is the possessor of heaven and earth, was quite aptly called God, the Highest, or Most High God. In the above scripture, the king of Salem (Jerusalem) blessed Abram in the name of the Most High God. Most High is not the name of the highest God. Therefore, if Most High is not the name of God, what is it?

What's really in a name? Does it matter what name we give anything or anyone? Seemingly, in today's world, a name no longer has any profound meaning or real significance. It has become nothing but a word used to denote famous or notorious persons.

To the ancients, however, a name was never taken lightly. Every name spoke volumes of its own. People named places and gave names to their children, which served to establish more of a personal relationship with them reflect some form of God consciousness or spiritual connotation. To the ancients, the bearer of a name was supposed to be "just like that name." In other words, if a name meant "good person," everybody expected the bearer of that name to be a good person.

In support of this, our Creator always ensured that anybody he employed to carry out a mission had a name that was reflective of the mission. In cases where he thought that their names were not reflective enough of their missions, he had them changed. One can find two wonderful examples of this in Genesis 17:5 and Genesis 32:24–30 (KJV).

In those two episodes, we see the changing of the name Abram to Abraham. Abram meant good and exalted father, and Abraham means father of a multitude. The Lord had plans to turn that good and exalted father into the father of many nations, hence, the name change. We also see the immediate renaming of another person from Jacob to Israel.

In the case of Jacob, what is most interesting is that after his name was changed, he demanded to know the name of the person with whom he wrestled. Jacob held that humanoid being to be God himself. Knowing the name of God puts one in a position of power and authority since they can now invoke his name at will. Jacob was so thrilled that he renamed the place where he had the encounter. He named the place Peniel, which means "face of God," for he truly believed that he had met and wrestled with God face-to-face.

Today, in the world of Christendom, the Creator of the heavens and the earth has become known simply as God and/or Jehovah. The practice of writing God with a capital "G" does not mean that God is the personal name of the God who created all things. On the other hand, Jehovah is not the proper name that our God has given himself.

I have deduced from my research that many biblical scholars share the view that the so-called name Jehovah is an unfounded name that is not rooted in the scriptures at all. Nevertheless, it has become a sacred name because of its repeated usage in hymns and religious songs. When I looked up the name Jehovah in *The Complete*

Biblical Library (a Hebrew-English Old Testament Dictionary), I discovered that Jehovah was not a real name. Jehovah is referred to as an artificially constructed name in *The Oxford Companion of the Bible*. In addition, *The Oxford Dictionary of the Christian Church* had no qualms with declaring that Jehovah is a bastard word. In the original Greek, Hebrew, and Aramaic texts, the name Jehovah was never mentioned at all! How did it find its way into the scriptures? Jehovah is a name that is made up of the consonants of a proper name and the vowels of a title.

Moreover, according to the widely acclaimed *Harper Collins Bible Dictionary*, the name Jehovah was only present in some versions of the Bible because of the translator's ignorance of the Hebrew language and customs.

Even today's religious scholars have rejected the so-called name Jehovah. And if those learned men have found the courage to denounce it openly and honestly as a name that was never mentioned in the original Hebrew, Greek, or Aramaic texts, why should anybody continue to utter that bastard word?

Jehovah is a theophoric name. It is simply a name that contains the bona fide name of the living God. And I will hasten here to say that even though it is not the proper name of our God, that is the reason why it has nevertheless been hallowed by usage in many popular reggae songs as well.

Joseph Hill, the leader of the reggae band Culture, wrote a popular song called "Rally Round Jah Throne." And as he sings that song, he says, "Rally round Jehovah's throne." Clearly, Jehovah sounds like *Jahovah*! Remember, Jehovah only contains the name, but it is not the proper name of our God.

Judah, Jeremiah, Isaiah, Abijah, and Elijah are very good biblical examples of names that also contains the sacred name of our God, but like the name Jehovah, they are not names of our God.

After spending decades exercising himself in ancient wisdom and godliness, we find Moses asking God about his personal name (Exodus 3:13–15 KJV). Obviously, he was not satisfied that the

Almighty had only made himself known to him verbally in the theophany of the burning bush. Without knowing his name, Moses felt as though he did not even know him at all.

> "When I come unto the children of Israel," Moses asked, "And shall say unto them, the God of your fathers have sent me ... and they shall say ... What is his name?' What shall I say unto them?" (Exodus 3:13 KJV)

The Lord made a personal identification to Moses:

> I AM That I AM ... say ... I AM has sent me. (Exodus 3:14 KJV)

In other words, our Lord said, 'I am He who is; that Almighty God who has been in existence forever, and I will be what I am, that great God; I will show you who I am by what I will do for them.'

As Moses tried to comprehend what he was hearing coming from the burning bush, God said, "Say ... the LORD God of your fathers ... has sent me ... this is my name forever" (Exodus 3:15 KJV).

Please note that the title Lord was written with all uppercase letters. Again, that is an indication as to where the proper name of our God was once written in the original Hebrew Bible before Babylon removed it.

All indications are that Moses was not quite satisfied with that response. He was not convinced that his people would believe that the God of their ancestors had appeared to him and revealed his sacred name.

After he fled Egypt due to the death of the Egyptian taskmaster, he sought refuge in the land of Midian. While there, he met and married the daughter of the priest, Jethro, who was also known as Reuel. Jethro became Moses's spiritual counsellor and advisor in secular things. As a priest, he must have known the name of the Almighty.

From all accounts, the Midianites were idolaters, and Jethro had come out from among them and separated himself to the Lord.

It was through Jethro that Moses learned about the true name of God whom he encountered in the burning bush many years later. Remember, Moses grew up in Egypt where there were many lords and gods.

To put an end to Moses's wavering, our Lord, in, Jerusalem version of the Bible, emphatically declared, "I am YHWH ... To Abraham ... I appeared as El Shaddai (Almighty), but I did not make my name, YHWH, known" (Exodus 6:2–3).

In the King James version of the scripture, that same piece of scripture reads: "I am the LORD ... to Abraham ... I appeared by the name of God Almighty, but by my name Jehovah was I not known" (Exodus 6:2–3 KJV).

The name YHWH was replaced with the title LORD (written with uppercase letters) and the artificially constructed name Jehovah.

In the *Metaphysical Bible Dictionary* (332), it is written that the name Jehovah was "incorrectly translated as the Lord." It also indicated that it was inserted wherever the proper name of our God was written in the original Hebrew text! And it is my belief that that was intentionally done to hide—if not to remove—our Lord's name from the scriptures altogether.

Remember, that it is the name they never wanted us to know, and one cannot truly call upon the name—as the scriptures encourages us to do—if one does not know the name. Knowing the name of our God gives us power and authority. We no longer need a priest or other human being to intercede for us since every man and woman can now boldly come before the throne of grace and call upon the name of God for themselves.

Interestingly, some scholars believe that when the Creator said, "But by my name, YHWH, was I not known to them" (Exodus 6:3, Jerusalem Bible), he was simply posing a rhetorical question to Moses. In other words, the Creator, while reasoning with Moses, asked, "But by my name, YHWH, was I not known to them?"

It is this writer's humble opinion that our Lord did, in fact, pose a rhetorical question to Moses since he had already made his name known to man after Seth (who was born to replace Abel, whom Cain killed), begat a son whom he named Enoch:

> Then began men to call upon the name of YHWH.
> (Genesis 4:26, Jerusalem Bible)

In most versions of the scripture, the name, YHWH, was replaced with the title LORD in uppercase letters.

In the scriptures—I cannot help reaffirming this truth—wherever the title LORD is written with uppercase letters, it tells us exactly where the sacred name of our God was once written in the original Hebrew text.

In the original Hebrew text, also known as the *consonantal text*, the revealed sacred name (represented with English letters) is YHWH. Those four consonants are also known as the tetragrammaton (the four-letter name).

Some rabbinical scholars have likened the name YHWH to an old Hebrew verb, *haway*, which they regard as another form of the verb *hayah*, which happens to be the verb "to be" in English. Our Lord addressed Moses in the first person: "I AM That I AM" (Genesis 3:14 KJV).

It is important to know that there were no vowels in the ancient Hebrew alphabet. The alphabet was made up of twenty-two consonants, and that is why scholars referred to the original text as the consonantal text.

Some scholars hold that although vocalization of the ancient Hebrew language was unambiguous, the absence of vowels in its alphabet would have made it extremely difficult for anyone to pronounce the four-letter name. Notwithstanding that, many biblical scholars today believe the four-letter name could have been pronounced Yahweh or *Yahawah*. Yah is the constricted or shortened form of Yahweh. The four-letter name was pronounced Yahweh or

Yahawah simply because there is no letter *J* in the ancient Hebrew alphabet.

I have deduced from *The Expository Dictionary of Bible Words* that pronouncing the four-letter name as Yahweh is making a scholarly guess about what the name may have actually sounded like during an attempted pronunciation. The editors of the American Standard Bible also expressed similar sentiments, which implicates the profound lack of certainty when it comes to the pronunciation of the four-letter name YHWH.

Interestingly, after conceding that the name YHWH was perhaps pronounced Yahweh, Schofield made a false declaration that Yahweh is pronounced Jehovah in English. How can Yahweh ever be pronounced Jehovah in English? They also teach that Jehovah is usually written Lord in the KJV (see the footnote related to Exodus 6:3 and Exodus 34:6 in the New Scofield Reference Bible). It is my opinion that the views they have expressed therein are false and misleading. Why, in their wisdom, they did not simply ignore the KJV and insert Jehovah wherever the title LORD was written in capital letters?

King James's scholars did not replace the name Jehovah with the title LORD as Scofield indicated. It appears that they were so vigilant that they opted to preserve the capitalized form of the word LORD. Obviously, they had some insight as to why the title LORD was written in capital letters in certain places in the ancient documents. The rabbinical scholars inserted the vowels of the word Adonai (which means Lord in English) between the consonants, YHWH, and get the artificially constructed name: Jehovah.

Some biblical scholars who are well versed in the Kabala (the oral traditions of the ancient Hebrew people) accommodate other transliterations that render the four-letter name as JHWH. In medieval Latin, it is JHVH. The name was then pronounced Jahweh, and Jah is its constricted or shortened form. The lexicographers of the *Harper Collins Bible Dictionary* also shared that same sentiment, declaring Jahweh/Jah an equal transcription of Yahweh.

The makers of the *Illustrated Dictionary and Concordance of the Bible* have also declared that Jah is the shortened form of the sacred name Jahweh.

In addition, *Webster's Third New International Dictionary* proclaimed Jah to be a "captured variant of Yah." Therefore, who shall say nay to me? Who can tell this Rasta man that Jahweh/Jah is not the proper name of our God?

I, as Rastafari, do solemnly proclaim, Jahweh/Jah to be the preferred pronunciation of the revealed, proper name that our God has given to himself. The one who was, who still is, and who will always be: the unchangeable, self-existent, and omnipotent One.

> I am Jah: that is my name; and my glory will I not
> give to another, neither my praise to carved images.
> (Isaiah 42:8 JB)

And after all has been said and done, this is what our Lord said to Moses:

> I Am He who is ... You are to tell the Israelites
> Jah ... has sent me to you. That is my name ... and
> by this name [Jah] all generations should remember
> me. (Exodus 3:14–15 JB)

There is the truth regarding the proper name of the one God of creation. The God who created the heavens and the earth has declared that his personal name is Jah.

Whenever we read the scriptures (particularly the Old Testament) and see the title LORD and the word GOD written in uppercase letters, we should never hesitate to utter the name, Jah. Let us take the first verse of Psalm 100 (KJV) as an example. Instead of saying, "Make a joyful noise unto the LORD, all ye lands," we shall now say, "Make a joyful noise unto the Lord [Jah]," or "Make a joyful noise unto Jah, our Lord." Also, Psalm 100:3 (KJV) should read: "Know ye that the Lord [Jah], he is God." Take note that the title Lord no longer appears fully capitalized. In those two examples, one can also ignore the title Lord altogether and simply write the proper name, Jah. Remember, the title Lord was inserted wherever the name, Jah, was written in the ancient scrolls.

When Jethro saw that Moses, his son-in-law, had truly brought the Israelites out of Egyptian slavery, he shouted, "Blessed be the LORD [Jah] … Now I know that the LORD [Jah] is greater than all gods" (Exodus 18:10–11 KJV).

When Eyesus (Jesus), the Hebrew-Israelite Christ, stood up in the temple and read from the book of the prophet Isaiah, he no doubt uttered the name Jahweh/Jah. Luke said that when he opened the book, he read from Isaiah 61:1. In the KJV, it is written: "The spirit of the Lord GOD is upon me, because the LORD has anointed me." Please take note that the title Lord appeared twice, but only when it appeared next to the word God (which was fully capitalized) and that it was not written with all uppercase letters. Lord was fully capitalized when it occurred the second time.

Clearly, the book of the prophet, Isaiah, which was handed to Eyesus in the temple, still had the sacred name, Jah, enshrined therein.

Here is what Eyesus boldly read:

> The spirit of the Lord GOD [Jah] is upon me, because the LORD [Jah] has anointed me. (Isaiah 61:1 KJV).

Unfortunately, when the actual book of Luke was written many, many years after Eyesus left the earth, the sacred name of our Lord was conveniently left out from the scriptures. And the translators did not even take the care to use uppercase letters to indicate where the proper name of our Lord was written in the ancient text.

Sadly, if Eyesus were to read from the book of Luke as we know it today, one would never hear him mention the proper name of God because it has been removed from the New Testament. That is exactly what the enemies of righteousness intended. Eyesus would utter the title Lord instead, and Lord is not the proper name of our LORD. This is what he would say:

> The spirit of the Lord is upon me, because he has
> anointed me. (Luke 4:18 KJV).

Please note that this time, the title Lord was not written with all uppercase letters. Our learned scribes have taken the name of the Lord, Jah, out of the New Testament. What a shame!

In the original text, Jahweh/Jah was written more than 6,800 times. In the Psalms alone, it was written more than 580 times. Not even once was the so-called name Jehovah written!

Henceforward, I shall not cease to invoke the sacred name of our God, and Lord, Jah, in this piece of writing.

During the second and third century BCE, there was a growing consensus among rabbinical scholars that the name JHVH/YHWH was too sacred or holy to be written—let alone to be uttered by sinful men. And for fear that it would be taken in vain and profaned, they substituted the Hebrew word Adonay/Adonai, which means Lord in English. And from thenceforward, anyone who was fortunate enough to read the known scriptures was told to say Lord whenever the sacred name Jahweh occurred.

Those rabbinical scholars misconstrued Exodus 20:7 (KJV): "Thou shall not take the name of the LORD thy God in vain; for the LORD, will not hold him guiltless that taketh his name in vain."

Again, the above quoted piece of scripture in the original text would have read: "Thou shall not take the name of Jah, thy God in vain; for Jah, will not hold him guiltless that taketh his name in vain."

Clearly, it is the name Jah that those infidels do not want us to utter at all! Uttering the sacred name reverently does not and cannot constitute "in vain." And that is why the scriptures said it is okay for us to call upon the name of the Lord. Yes, the people who are called by his name must also call upon and declare his holy name, Jah. Today, the Rasta man is the only man out here in modern Babylon who calls upon the name Jah.

Some Bible scholars believe that the unscriptural practice of substituting the sacred name Jah with the title Lord was conceived during the late Middle Ages—and that Christians misunderstood why that was done in the first place. Hundreds of years earlier, rabbinical scholars had already blotted out the sacred name, Jah, and replaced it with the word Adonay/Adonai, which means Lord in English. Many centuries after vowel points were introduced into the Hebrew language to aid in vocalization, the religious authorities simply inserted the vowels of Adonay/Adonai between the consonants of the sacred four-letter name and came up with the name Jehovah. Not one of the Bible prophets knew the name Jehovah. Eyesus (Jesus) never uttered it either.

Although that practice regained popularity as early as AD 1100, volume six of the *Anchor Bible Dictionary*, accredited it to Petrus Galatinus (1460–1540). Petrus was a renowned Roman Catholic theologian, philosopher, and confessor to Pope Leo X. Around AD 1518, he quite arbitrarily inserted the vowels of Adonay/Adonai between the consonants of the four-letter name, JHWH/JHVH, and the bastard word (Jehovah) popped up (see diagrams below).

```
A  D  O  N  A  Y          A  D  O  N  A  I
   ↓     ↓     ↓              ↓     ↓     ↓
   ↓     ↓     ↓              ↓     ↓     ↓
   ↓     ↓     ↓              ↓     ↓     ↓
Y  A  H  O  W  A  H       J  A  H  O  V  A  H
*     *     *     *          *     *     *     *
```

Now, can you recognize the four-letter name at all? In fact, if you were to remove the word Adonay along with the lines that show where the vowels were inserted between the four consonants, all that is left would be the artificially constructed name Yahowah/Jahovah. That is the name that some misinformed theologians have given to the God who created the sun, the moon, and the stars after they blotted out the proper name that he gave himself. Clearly, the confessor misconstrued the noble intention that the rabbinical scholars had in mind when they added vowel points to the consonantal writings.

In 1604, King James—in his capacity as head of the Church of England—commissioned a group of fifty-four independent scholars to translate the Bible into English. Remarkably, they only used the name Jehovah four times (Exodus 6:3, Psalm 83:18, Isaiah 12:2, and Isaiah 26:4) in the KJV. That is remarkable since it is believed that they adopted well over 75 percent of the work of the sixteenth-century scholar and translator William Tyndale (1494–1536).

Tyndale is believed to have been the first person to translate the scriptures into English, a feat that earned him the name "father of the English Bible." After a rather unpleasant encounter with a Roman Catholic priest, Tyndale vowed to make the scriptures accessible to the common man who spoke English, a language which was still in the vernacular. Allegedly, Tyndale became outraged after the priest suggested that people would be do better if they heeded the words of the pope rather than God. Remember, the masses of people were not supposed to know the scriptures, save, of course, that which the pope wanted them to know.

Tyndale had the New Testament translated by 1526, and the first five books of the Old Testament, also known as the Torah, were available by 1530—eighty-one years before the KJV of 1611. After examining pertinent portions of his work, it became clear that he was unaware of the substitution that was made many centuries earlier. As might be expected, he employed the name *Iehouah* (Jehovah) in place of Jahweh. King James's translators adopted Iehouah as Lord, which

Scofield wrongly said means Jehovah in English. Clearly, it was a case of the blind leading the blind.

While commenting on his knowledge and ability to accurately translate the scriptures from the original Hebrew text, one dealer of rare and antique Bibles remarked that Tyndale may have known very little about the Hebrew language. And that's exactly what Harper Collins referred to as the translator's ignorance of the Hebrew language and customs.

Could Tyndale's elementary knowledge of the Hebrew language have been the reason some thirty thousand changes were made to King James's version of the Bible shortly after its publication in 1611? Also, could that have lead Noah Webster, the famous author and dictionary maker—in his very own translation of the English Bible in 1833—to correct another 150 words that he thought were wrong or misleading?

It is my opinion that because King James' translators relied so heavily on Tyndale's work, they repeated his mistakes regarding the sacred name. Nevertheless, there is no doubt in my mind that it was divine guidance that ordered the king's translators to retain the sacred name Jah in the Bible. In fact, it's the only place in the entire KJV of the Bible that the sacred name Jah is literally written: "Extol him who rideth upon the heavens by his name, Jah" (Psalm 68:4 KJV).

As might be expected, in the New Scofield Reference Bible, that same piece of scripture wrongly reads: "Extol him who rideth upon the heavens by his name, which is the LORD" (Psalm 68:4, New Scofield Reference Bible). Have you noticed that Scofield replaced the sacred name with the title Lord? Unwilling to write the bona fide name, Scofield (perhaps unawares) simply capitalized the entire title Lord, which they say means Jehovah. Remember, whenever the title Lord appears in full capital letters that tells us exactly where the proper name, Jah, was once written in the ancient text.

Surprisingly (and without contention) when referring to this piece of scripture, Scofield boldly agreed (in the footnote) that it was written as Jah in the KJV.

A very interesting article in *Watchtower* magazine from July 1, 2010 was entitled "Do you know God by name?" The writer, most truthfully, acknowledged that there is a difference between a name and a title of honor. Unfortunately, that writer declared that we must get to know him by the artificially constructed name, Jehovah, and I think that he knows better. He is willing to let sleeping dogs lie rather than admit the gospel truth. It is an attitude of having been preaching a lie for so long now that it would be too shameful to admit the truth.

Notwithstanding those facts, many critics have voiced their qualms about the sacred name Jah because there is no "J" in the Hebrew alphabet. There is, however, an internationally accepted process or standard whereby one transliterates letters and words from one alphabet or language into another without changing pronunciation. That process is commonly known as *anglicization*.

Translators and language experts agree that one need not be too concerned about the absence of one letter or the other in any given alphabet—but rather about the variations that occur due to the similarity in sound produced by different letters during pronunciation. For example, doesn't the letter C as used in the word cat convey a distinct "K" sound?

Again, herein lie the greatest obstacle that translators had to surmount: the original Hebrew language had no vowels, and experts say that in many languages, people spell words based on the sound of their vowels. It is my opinion that this is the main reason rabbinical scholars forbid the uttering of the four-letter name. They were not sure how to pronounce the four-letter name; therefore, they simply told the people to be on the safe side (in fear of uttering blasphemy) and say "Lord" instead.

Vowels were introduced into the Hebrew language by a group of scholars known as the Masoretes or transmitters of the scriptures. They were highly regarded as the scribes of their day and were, therefore, charged with the responsibility of preserving the consonantal text. Their work later became known as the Masoretic text. They introduced Hebrew vowels into the consonantal text to aid their community in the pronunciation of words and to remind readers to substitute Adonai for Lord. In other words, whenever you meet the sacred name Jah while reading the scriptures—if they have not yet blotted the name out of the scroll or book you happen to be reading from—do not utter the name Jah. You are to use the title Lord instead. In effect, what they were saying, "People, you are not supposed to call upon the name of Jah, our God."

Imagine some fanatical rabbinical scholars encouraging God's people not to utter his name at all! How can anyone blaspheme? How can they take the name Jah in vain when they reverently utter it where he inspired it to be written in the scripture? Also, teaching that the name was too holy to be uttered is foolishness. It is my belief that they believed that the masses of people should never get to know the sacred name. In my mind, that amounts to religious bigotry.

The imposition of vowels into the consonantal text had far-reaching consequences, and in fact, it contributed to the Christian misunderstanding during the late Middle Ages. The original Hebrew alphabet only had twenty-two letters, all of which were consonants. In the English alphabet, there are twenty-one consonants and five vowels that aid in anglicization as well as vocalization.

Educators say that the letter *A*, in the English alphabet has more than a dozen pronunciations. In the German alphabet, the letter *J* is pronounced like the letter *Y* in English. One can now appreciate why Jah is an alternate transcription of Yah.

Notwithstanding the absence of the letter *J* in the Hebrew language, so-called rabbinical scholars were satisfied to approve names such as Jerusalem, Jacob, Jeremiah, Jesus, and even Judas.

The truth is that it is only when it comes to the mentioning of the sacred name, Jah, that the issue of the letter *J* is being highlighted—as though the name should never be mentioned at all. Whenever I talk with someone who is aware of this truth, their first reaction has always been to ask, "Don't you know that there is no letter *J* in the Hebrew alphabet? They are not at all concerned about the name Yah or all the other names of people and places in the scriptures that begin with the letter *J*. They simply don't want to hear about the name Jah.

Again, it is my belief that those rabbinical scholars attempted to eliminate the sacred name Jah altogether. It must never be known to the masses of people—lest they invoke his name at will. Could that have been the reason the Roman Catholic priest told William Tyndale that the people would do better with the pope's word than with God's?

Again, it is written in Isaiah 42:8, in the Jerusalem version of the Bible: "I am Jah: that is my name." The scriptures said that Seth—the son of Adam who replaced Abel, whom Cain killed—and his son, Enoch, were the first men to call upon the name Jah. (Genesis 4:26 KJV).

David also wrote in Psalm 22:22 (KJV): "I will declare thy name unto my brethren." Clearly, he knew the sacred name—or he could not have declared it. He also wrote in Psalm 99:6 (KJV): "Moses and Aaron … among those who call upon his name; they called upon the LORD [Jah], and he answered them."

The psalmist must have taken the utmost care when he penned that piece of scripture. He said that they called upon his name. And what name did they call upon? They called upon the name Jah.

During my youthful days, Pastor Phillip Richards remarked during a Bible study meeting, that the sacred name Jah was only present in Psalm 68:4 of the KJV because of an error in translation. His remark came after a young lady named, Francine, shouted, "The Rasta man God, Jah!"

He simply could not bring himself to admit that Jah, as King David aptly said, is God. He refused to honor the sacred name because the Rasta man loved it and declared it publicly. He probably felt that if he openly honored the name Jah that he was associating himself with the Rasta man who, in those days, was treated as the outcast of society.

Until the advent of the Rasta man, the sacred name Jah had been labeled forbidden by some religious scholars who believed in letting sleeping dogs lie. The first person I ever heard uttering the sacred name Jah was a Rasta man. In fact, it was a Rasta man who let me know that the name Jah was written in the Bible. Today, it has become like music to our ears.

The scripture entreats us to call upon the name of our God. Our God said that his proper name is Jah; therefore, let us all call upon his name. Let it be known that calling upon the name of our God, Jah, does not mean taking his name in vain.

Like all other languages, the ancient Hebrew language has evolved. In today's Hebrew language, the proper name of God is יהוה. In the alphabet of biblical Hebrew, the letter, ה is named Hey, ו is called Waw, and י is known as Yod.

The name, יהוה should be spelled from the right to the left (see diagram).

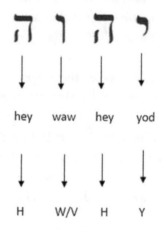

After the rabbinical scholars substituted the title Lord for the proper name, יהוה, they suddenly realized that in the original text, the name sometimes, literally, occurred next to the actual word, Lord, in certain portions of scripture. In Genesis 15:2 (KJV), Moses wrote, "And Abram (Abraham) said, Lord GOD, what will thou give me." The words Adonay (Lord) and YHWH/JHVH (God) were used alongside each other. After realizing they could not substitute the name with Adonay again, they simply wrote God (Elohim). In the KJV, there are more than 250 instances where the proper name Jah was arbitrarily translated as God (Genesis 15:8; Exodus 34:6; Psalm 69:6; and Isaiah 7:7 KJV).

The *Anchor Bible Dictionary* (vol. 6, 1011–1012) cites archaeological evidence of the use of the sacred name Jah in Syria as early as 1400 BC. In addition, the *Complete Biblical Library* (485) also cited archaeological evidence from two hundred years before the time of Abraham! Abraham lived around 2200–2100 BC.

One can now understand why a group of contentious Jews sought to kill Eyesus (Jesus) after he declared, "Before Abraham was, I AM" (John 8:58 KJV).

Not only was he claiming to be one with God, Jah, he was also declaring his name to those hypocritical scribes and Pharisees who also believed that the name should never be uttered.

Again, in his high priestly prayer, shortly before his Crucifixion, he uttered, "I have declared unto them thy name and will declare it" (John 17:26 KJV).

All indications are that Eyesus never ceased to openly utter the name Jah. From the tender age of twelve to the very moment before his execution, he uttered the name Jah.

As mentioned before, while expounding Isaiah 61:1 (JB) to the great teachers of the Jews in the temple at Jerusalem, he boldly declared the name Jah. Luke penned it in chapter 4 of his book.

In as much as our learned rabbinical scholars attempted to remove the sacred name, Jah, from the scriptures, they were honest enough to tell us that they substituted the words Lord and God, Elohim. That is why a Jewish authority on the Torah suggested that the substitution was made to remind the people to say Lord/God. The masses of people were not supposed to declare the name Jah. They never thought we would come to know the sacred name of our God.

Have you ever wondered why the people who were present at Calvary remarked that Eyesus was calling upon Elijah? And do you know that they were expecting the old prophet to come to his rescue?

When Eyesus cried, "Eli, Eli" (Matthew 27:46 KJV), all that they heard was, "Eli, Jah, Eli, Jah," which is to say, "My God, Jah, my God, Jah!" One must also remember that Matthew had not yet written the book of Matthew that we have today. Obviously, they all knew that the very name Elijah was no ordinary, meaningless name. The name Elijah literally means "my God is Jah," or "Jah is my God." Further, they all knew from Jesus's declaration that his God, our God, is Jah. Yes, Jah is our God!

One of the most remarkable Bible stories in defense of the sacred name Jah is that of the prophet Elijah and his encounter with King Ahab (the seventh king of Israel) and his idolatrous wife, Jezebel. Ahab reigned from about 874–852 BC. He was the son of Omri, the king of the northern kingdom of Israel.

Without any qualms, Elijah told everybody that his God was Jah, also known as a "hairy man," which is to say a Rasta man! Obviously, that is because of the locks of the hair, the consecration of his God, our God, Jah upon his head.

Because of his zeal and love for Jah, he was also known as the fiery prophet. To most people —including King Ahaziah, who became king of Israel after the death of Ahab—he was known simply as the hairy man or the Rasta man.

From the very moment that the king's messengers gave the hairy man's description to him about a man who had turned them back with a message, the king knew it was Elijah—and a dreadful feeling overshadowed him. His heart quaked! His day of judgment had arrived.

Upon the request of his newlywed, Jezebel, and as an act to mark the deepening political ties between himself and her father, Ethbaal, king of the Sidonians, Ahab embraced idol worship in Israel. He proclaimed Baal, the Phoenician goddess of war and fertility—whom the Sidonians also worship under the name Ashtoreth—to be the new god of Israel.

The name Ethbaal speaks about the king's devotion to his newfound idol god, Baal, and because of the promise of fertility and prosperity in the fields, the children of Israel were easily lured into idolatry.

During those days, marriage between the Sidonians and the Israelites was forbidden (1 Kings 11:1–2 KJV). Marriage was forbidden not because of so-called race but because those people (the Sidonians) were idolaters. Therefore, for one to say that marriage was forbidden because of ethnicity is a promotion of racism and religious bigotry.

Our God, Jah, made one race, and that is humanity. He warned his people who esteemed him as the one and only true God:

> For surely they (the idolatrous) will turn away your
> heart after their gods. (1 Kings 11:2 KJV)

Therefore, from the moment Elijah heard about the marriage between the king of Israel and Jezebel, the daughter of the Sidonian king, he knew that his people had become idolatrous; that is what infuriated him.

It is written that Ahab "did evil in the sight of the LORD [Jah] above all who were before him ... he went and served Baal, and worshiped him ... he made an idol; and he did more to provoke the LORD [Jah], God of Israel, to anger than all the kings who were before him" (1 Kings 16:30–33 KJV).

After an encounter with the king, Elijah ordered a severe drought upon the land to convince the people that Jah alone is God. For three years and six months, the drought wreaked havoc upon the land, and the Sidonian goddess of rain and fertility proved herself to be a useless, dead god.

Elijah openly challenged Ahab in a contest to prove who served the true God. As might be expected, Ahab's false god could not respond to his people's request for fire from heaven to consume a bullock prepared for an offering. On the other hand, Jah responded promptly to Elijah's prayer; fire descended from above and consumed the bullock, which he prepared as a burnt offering.

Here is an excerpt of his prayer:

> LORD [Jah], God of Abraham ...
> Let them know that you are God ...
> And that I am your servant ...
> Answer me, O LORD [Jah] answer me that this
> people may know
> That you, LORD [Jah] is God. (1 Kings 18:36–
> 37 KJV)

> When all the people saw this they fell on their faces,
> and they said, "The Lord [Jah] is God; the LORD
> [Jah] is God." (1 Kings 18:39 KJV)

The fiery ones' fury did not end there; the very thought of those deceptive teachers of idolatry walking free taunted him even more. On that same day, the waters of the brook, Kishon, turned red with blood. He had them all put to death there.

Unquestionably, Jah, is the personal, revealed name of the God of creation. It seems to me that in times past, the religious pundits thought we should never know that. Therefore they tried to hide the name right before our eyes. They insisted that we must not call upon the proper name of our God—but rather upon an artificially constructed name that contains the name but is not the name itself.

After hundreds of years of slavery in the so-called New World, the descendants of the Hebrew-Israelites who Moses left behind— and whose progenies have survived the African Holocaust—has again come to know the proper name of their God. Let us, therefore, call upon the name of our God. If we do not call upon his name, he will not acknowledge us. For too long, we have been calling upon the Lord, God, and fooling ourselves, thinking that we were calling upon our Lord, Jah:

> Blessed be the name of the LORD [Jah] from this
> time forth and for evermore. (Psalm 113:2 KJV)

While he was in the spirit on Patmos, John, the aging apostle of Eyesus, wrote: "And I heard ... the voice of a great multitude ... saying, Allelujah [Hallelujah]" (Revelation 19:6 KJV). Those words John heard coming out of the throne of the Highest—the voice of those who chose—and were chosen to honor, praise, and exalt the sacred name of our God, Jah.

In closing, it is expedient to remind us what our Creator said to Moses:

> Say unto the children of Israel, the LORD [Jah]
> the God of your fathers ... has sent me ... this is my
> name forever, and by this name, [Jah], all generations
> should remember me. (Exodus 3:15, JB)

Selah.

Chapter 2

The Second Coming

IT IS MY belief that the entire world of Christendom has, up to this day, misconstrued the true meaning of the term "Second Coming" as it relates to the return of Eyesus Kristos (Jesus Christ), the Hebrew-Israelite Christ, to this earth.

In cultures where the Bible has had prevailing influence, people are still looking steadfastly toward heaven for the day when time will stand still, the dark clouds in the sky will be rolled back, an innumerable number of white, fluffy-winged humanoid beings will emerge, blowing long, slender golden trumpets, and Eyesus will suddenly reappear. Such a brilliant display of the Second Coming does not seem to be in keeping with what the scripture teaches, but that is exactly what Christians teach today.

In the holy scriptures, the Second Coming has been typified or likened to that of a thief in the night. No thief comes in pomp and glory. The thief comes unawares and takes you by surprise. Only after he has made his escape with your prized possession do you realize that your home has been burglarized.

It is this writer's humble opinion that the Second Coming of Eyesus has already taken place—and it took place in similar manner to his first coming/advent. And one cannot truly understand the true meaning of the term Second Coming unless one knows what a coming/advent really means in biblical terms.

Today, we refer to the First Coming of the Messiah as the "incarnation of the Christ." In Latin, *incarnation* means "to become flesh," and becoming flesh simply means to be born or to become human:

> The Word was with God [Jah], and the Word was God [Jah] ... and the Word was made flesh and dwelt among us. (John 1:1, 14 KJV)

When he made his first advent, Eyesus did not come in pomp and glory; he did not come with the clouds of heaven as many were expecting him to. He "descended," he came through the biological process of conception, and he was born of a woman. He came into this world.

About five hundred years prior to the Word becoming flesh, the prophet Malachi made a prophecy:

> Behold, I will send you Elijah the prophet before the coming of the great and dreadful day of the LORD [Jah]. (Malachi 4:5 KJV)

And from that day Malachi uttered those words, all the people of Israel looked steadfastly for the visible, physical return of the old, hairy, dreadlocked prophet, Elijah. In effect, they anticipated his Second Coming! That prophesied coming of Elijah can only be referred to as his Second Coming since, as stated in the scriptures, he had been literally taken up into heaven hundreds of years earlier.

That became the most anticipated event that was to take place before the first advent of the Messiah. In fact, for many people, the Second Coming of Elijah was even more important than the actual coming of Messiah because if Elijah did not come at all, then the Messiah would not come either:

> Elijah must first come. (Matthew 17:10 KJV)

By that time, the only two persons known to have ascended into heaven (as recorded in the scripture) were Enoch, the Ethiopian, and the prophet Elijah. *The Oxford Dictionary of the Christian Church* referred to the "Assumption of Moses" (dated around the middle of the first century AD), which claimed that Moses had also ascended into heaven.

Could that be the reason the scripture said that nobody knew where he was buried? It is this writer's belief that that is also the reason the devil and Michael the archangel disputed about the body of Moses in the Bible (Jude 9 KJV).

Neither Enoch nor Elijah experienced physical death:

Enoch walked with God [Jah] and he was not; for God took him. (Genesis 5:24 KJV)

Elijah was taken up into heaven with a great show. There was that fiery chariot drawn by horses of fire as well as a tornado-like whirling wind. Also, there was an enthusiastic crowd of fifty people who watched from the opposite side of the Jordan River as he ascended, leaving his successor, Elisha, gazing steadfastly into the sky (2 Kings 2:11 KJV). There is, therefore, no doubt that all of Israel would have been expecting Elijah to come again in like manner as some had seen him go into heaven.

Many centuries passed, and then came a strange man whose asceticism manifested itself in his wilderness-style garment, which he fashioned from the skin of the beast of burden, and in his diet of locusts and wild honey. That man was also a magnetic leader; large crowds would gather around him daily to hear his message of social justice and to seize the opportunity to be immersed by him in the Jordan River. They somehow knew that his baptism of repentance for the remission of sins was somewhat different from their traditional animal sacrifices, ritual baths, and washings.

People from all walks of life, even military personnel and the notorious tax collectors, after hearing that the "axe is already laid unto the root of the tree" (Luke 3:9 KJV), felt the need to make changes in their lives.

Interestingly, some Bible scholars hold that the baptizer did baptize in that same section of the River Jordan that the prophet Elijah parted just before he was taken up into heaven, hundreds of years earlier.

As might be expected, the baptizer soon became a person of great concern to both the religious and the political authorities alike. They could not understand why so many people were following that strange man around. The large crowds he drew made King Herod very uneasy. He must have seen him as a direct threat to national security and the political stability of the state.

The first disciples of Eyesus Kristos (Jesus Christ) were disciples of that same man who was baptizing people in the River Jordan. Those two disciples—Peter and his brother Andrew—began to follow Jesus soon after he began his public ministry.

Surprise took the religious authorities, and they felt marginalized. If the baptizer came from the Lord, Jah, howbeit that they of the sect of the Pharisees, being the rulers of the Jews, were not a part of this religious revival? Consequently, they sent a delegation of priests and Levites from the temple at Jerusalem to confront the baptizer.

One of the very first questions posed to him was this: "Are you Elijah?" (John 1:21 KJV). However, all indications are that they all knew who he was. They knew him to be John, the son of a former priest, Zacharias. The Lord, Jah, had blessed Zacharias with that special son when he was a very old man. John was born while his father was still a priest at the temple in Jerusalem.

In his capacity as priest, Zacharias would have made known to his colleagues the encounter he had with the angel, Gabriel, before the birth of his son, John.

An angel is a humanoid messenger of Jah. The messenger stood on the right side of the altar of incense and told Zacharias that his aging wife would bear him a son whom the Lord has already called to his service to be the forerunner of the promised Messiah:

He shall be filled with the Holy Spirit ... and he
shall go before him in the spirit and power of Elijah.
(Luke 1:15–17 KJV)

The angel told Zacharias that the same spirit and power of the
Highest that was upon the fiery prophet, Elijah, shall also be upon
his son, John.

Zacharias, as priest, was familiar with the prophetic words of
Malachi:

Behold, I will send you Elijah, the prophet, before
the coming of the great and dreadful day of the
LORD [Jah]. (Malachi 4:5 KJV)

And like everyone else, he was longing for the day when Elijah would
come and restore all things.

The notion that the prophet Elijah could have returned in the
personality of John the baptizer baffled the learned Pharisees. They
could not go forward to Jerusalem without an answer straight from
the horse's mouth. The matter was far too important to them; it was
like a death-or-life issue. Hence the question: Are you Elijah? cannot
go unanswered.

John did not entertain the thought that he was Elijah who was
to come, neither could he overstand why others thought that he was.
He completely denied that he was Elijah. I do believe, however, that
John knew the prophets; he knew what they had prophesied many
centuries earlier.

John grew up in a household where his parents were said to be
"both righteous before God [Jah], walking in all the commandments
and ordinances of the Lord blameless" (Luke 1:6 KJV). His father's
main function in the temple was to burn incense in the holy place,
a priest's office that required uprightness. The holy place, which
contained the table of showbread, lampstand and the altar of incense,
was located just outside the entrance to the holy of holies. No unholy

person could approach the altar of incense, and that is the reason the scripture described Zacharias as a blameless man.

Although he was unwilling to blow his own trumpet, John declared himself to be "the voice of [the] one crying in the wilderness" (John 1:23 KJV). John also knew that the voice crying in the wilderness would have had to be that of the promised forerunner of the Messiah and that that person would have been none other than the prophet Elijah (Malachi 4:5 KJV). Therefore, by admitting that he was "a voice crying in the wilderness," he also admitted (probably unknowingly) that he was the prophet Elijah who was to come.

After hearing about the imprisonment of John the Baptist, Eyesus confirmed that John the Baptist was Elijah who was to come, which Matthew documented:

> For this is he of whom it is written, Behold I send my messenger ... And if you will receive it, this is Elijah who was to come. (Matthew 11:10, 14 KJV)

Just before Eyesus unequivocally declared that John the Baptist was Elijah who was to come, he said, "And if you will receive it." In other words, I know that this truth, which I am about to reveal to you, will be hard for you to digest; it will make you question everything that you were taught, but it's the naked truth.

In addition, Eyesus rebuked three of his disciples shortly after his transfiguration for questioning whether Elijah had truly returned:

> And his disciples asked ... Why then say the Scribes that Elias [Elijah] must first come? And Eyesus answered ... Elijah truly shall first come ... But I say unto you that, Elijah has come already, and they knew him not ... Then the disciples under[over] stood that he spoke unto them of John the Baptist. (Matthew 17:10–13 KJV)

In Matthew chapters 11 and 17, Eyesus (Jesus), without any qualms, declared that the prophet, Elijah had returned (he had his Second Coming) just like the prophets said he would. Moreover, he also made it abundantly clear that Elijah returned in the personality of none other than John the Baptist. He did not descend from the sky in a fiery chariot as the people had seen him go. He had his Second Coming in like manner as they had seen him go. He ascended in the flesh, and he returned in the flesh, born of a woman. Also, when Eyesus first declared (in chapter 11) that John was Elijah who they were looking for, he added, "He that has ears to hear, let him hear" (Matthew 11:15 KJV).

Eyesus cautioned that some people will never come to know the truth. Some people will reject the truth simply because they cannot bring themselves to accept the messenger. They will accept truth only if Mr. Tom told them so.

His disciples were not at all perturbed because he did give them the assurance that "unto them it was given to know the mysteries of the kingdom of heaven" (Matthew 13:11 KJV).

After John the Baptist was born, his father said:

> And you, child, shall be called the prophet of the
> Highest: for you shall go before the face of the Lord,
> [Jah], to prepare his ways. (Luke 1:76 KJV)

John, the disciple of Eyesus, attested to that prophecy many years later:

> There was a man sent from God, [Jah], whose name
> was John. The same came for a witness, to bear
> witness of the Light. (John 1:6–7 KJV)

Unfortunately, his mission was cut short. His message of social justice and his condemnation of immorality in high places landed him behind bars, and he was beheaded.

35

Whether it's someone's first or second coming or arrival into this world, our Lord (Jah) has ordained from creation that it takes place through the known biological process, which begins at conception and ends (everything else being equal) when the mother gives birth to her child. That is exactly how Eyesus (Jesus) came (descended) to this earth the first time.

And if you will receive it now, that is the biblical definition of an advent, a coming (whether it's a first or second) into this world. The coming in like manner as ye have seen him go into heaven has nothing to do with an outward show. It pertains to the actual way our God, Jah, affects these comings by the manifestation of that same spirit and power that possessed the one who departed into the personality of another.

I believe that we can now appreciate why it took the disciples of Eyesus a while before they realized that he told them that the same spirit and power that was upon Elijah was now upon John the Baptist, and that Elijah had returned in the personality of John.

John's mother was six months pregnant with him when her cousin, Mary, told her that she was also pregnant with Eyesus. At that very moment, John/Elijah leaped for joy in his mother's womb (Luke 1:41 KJV).

Throughout scripture, many writers have made full usage of symbolism as a teaching aid. Take, for example, the expressions "beast coming up from the sea" and "coming with or in clouds of heaven." The writer used beast to denote world leaders and their kingdoms as well as other notorious persons who would rise up to worsen the plight of humankind. The sea was indicative of the masses of people on the earth.

Similarly, a cloud was used to denote a multitude of people or resurrected saints. In many instances, it was used as a theophanic symbol to indicate the presence of the Lord, Jah. Let us take the theophanic cloud mentioned in Exodus 13:21 (KJV) as an example. There, the Lord made his presence known by means of the pillar of cloud during the daytime and by the fiery cloud during the night.

During the day, the cloud gave covering and shade, and at night, the fiery cloud gives light and warmth.

The *Dictionary of Biblical Imagery* agrees that clouds represent the hiddenness of Jah and serve as a constant reminder of the mystery that surrounds him. In Leviticus 16:2 (KJV), the Lord told Moses that when he sees a cloud upon the mercy seat, he will know that he, the Lord, (Jah) is in that cloud.

Now, as a prelude to his Second Coming, Eyesus said, "When the son of man cometh, shall he find faith on the earth?" (Luke 18:8 KJV). When he makes his next appearance, will anybody recognize godhood in whomsoever he chooses to indwell? He was very concerned about his Second Coming; will they accept him as the returned Messiah or reject him again?

Since his ascension, his apostles, more than anybody, were looking for his return. And from the language and tone of the Gospels, one gets the feeling that they thought he would return during their lifetimes—even though Eyesus never gave them a date or time when he assured them that "he will come again and receive them unto himself" (John 14:3 KJV).

Although he was not there when Eyesus reasoned with the other disciples, Paul, in his letter to the Church at Corinth, said, "We shall not all sleep" (1 Corinthians 15:51 KJV). While addressing the Christians at Thessalonica, he wrote, "We who are alive and remain" (1 Thessalonians 4:15 KJV).

Paul relished the thought that he might have been physically alive when Eyesus was supposed to have staged his Second Coming by descending from the clouds in the sky. It is clear from the tone in his writings that he also believed that, at his Second Advent, Eyesus was going to literally burst out from the clouds in the sky,

Today, after more than two thousand years, the entire world of Christendom is still awaiting—and probably scoffing: "Where is the promise of his coming?" (2 Peter 3:4 KJV).

Many people, including William Miller and C. T. Russell have publicly made false predictions about the next coming of the Messiah.

Miller was a Seventh-day Adventist who boasted about his knowledge of scripture. In fact, he believed that one could take the scripture literally since it is its own interpreter. Miller would predict a date for the coming of the Messiah, and when that date passed without his appearance, he would simply set another date—none of which ever materialized. It is written in the *Seventh Day Encyclopedia* (73–75) that he once foretold that the Parousia or next pomp coming of the Messiah would take place in 1843. Probably under pressure from his followers for a more specific date, in January of 1843, he told them between March 21, 1843, and March 21, 1844. As might be expected, before March 21, 1844 came, he told them if the Messiah did not come, they should simply carry on with their daily lives until he comes.

Russell, a Jehovah's Witness lay preacher, told his congregation that Eyesus did, in fact, return to the earth in 1878, but that he came in an invisible form and was waiting until the battle of Armageddon, which was supposed to have taken place in 1914, before he sets up his throne upon the earth. That never materialized either. Nobody will ever know the exact year or month when the Messiah will make his appearance unless the Lord himself tells them.

Ethiopian legend said that as the 1890s dawned, astrologers (sacred scribes) in Ethiopia forewarned one, Ras Makonnen—the commander of the armed forces as well as chief advisor to the aging emperor, Menelik II—about a significant astrological event that was about to take place in that country. Like their biblical counterpart, it was not unusual for Ethiopians who hold high public office to consult with astrologers. The Bible refers to them as wise men or magi who took astrological events very seriously. In fact, astrological events were viewed as object lessons or messages from the Creator himself.

Many people in Ethiopia, including Archbishop Yesehaq, hold that one of the wise men, or magi, who saw and followed the star that led them to the Christ Child in Bethlehem, was an Ethiopian king who was also an astrologer. Yesehaq also acknowledged that historical records show that that a wise man was ruler around the time that Eyesus was supposedly born.

The wise men in Ethiopia foresaw a stellar configuration in which Neptune and Pluto were going to intersect each other's orbit, and that configuration would resonate positively upon the constellation of Leo, which rules the house of Judah. By way of interpretation, that stellar configuration meant that a bright star (a child) would be born to govern the people of Ethiopia at home and abroad.

Not long after, as fate would have it, Makonnen's wife, Wayzaro Yashimabet, conceived and gave birth to a male child. When interpreted, the name Wayzaro Yashimabet literally means "lady of a thousand." It is my belief that if Makonnen did not quote from the Bible for his wife, the portion of scripture which says, "Blessed art thou among women, and blessed is the fruit of thy womb" (Luke 1:42 KJV), then he probably said, "Amongst a thousand women, thou art blessed."

The child was born on July 23, 1892. Interestingly, that year in the Ethiopian calendar was also the year of John, the apostle of Eyesus Kristos. He was born into the ancient dynasty of Menelik I, the son of Makeda, the queen of Ethiopia (also known as the queen of Sheba) and the wise, black king, Solomon of Jerusalem. And that made him the true seed of David according to the flesh.

Could this be the return of the child who was "set for the fall and rising again of many … and for a sign which shall be spoken against?" (Luke 2:34 KJV). Moreover, could this be the righteous branch the Lord, Jah, did promise to raise to David? He was named Lidj Tafari Makonnen, but one day, when he was older, he told a priest that no one knew his proper name.

As fate would have it, about five years before the coming of Tafari, a man appeared in the Caribbean Basin. His name was Marcus (little hammer) Mosiah Garvey. Like John the Baptist, he bore a message of social justice, and he drew large crowds wherever he went. Pleading the cause of the poor and oppressed workingmen and workingwomen, the spirit of the Lord, Jah took him throughout the Caribbean, Europe, and as well as North, Central, and South America. He openly criticized the ill treatment meted out to workers, especially to those of African descent.

He taught that all the black Hebrew-Israelites who had recently been freed from slavery in the New World, and found themselves scattered throughout the earth, should purpose in their minds not to suffer any longer—and we can only improve our lot if we organize ourselves and decide to build our own nation in Africa. As might be expected, he also became a person of great concern to both the political and the religious authorities.

Remember, our colonial slavers and so-called religious authorities had all taken crafty council against us as they fulfilled the scripture:

> Come and let us cut them off from being a nation; that
> the name of Israel may be no more in remembrance.
> (Psalm 83:4 KJV)

Garvey knew that we are the only people on the face of the earth who, up to this day, cannot truly say that we are a nation. He became concerned that the black people had not developed themselves after more than 350 years in the West. Of all peoples, only the black man does not have a president or country to look after his wants and needs.

The political authorities saw him only as one sowing the seeds of discord and rebellion, and hence a threat to their country's economic stability, political stability, and national security. They had him under constant surveillance; he was also shot, and like John the Baptist, he held fast to his message of social justice, which landed him behind bars in the United States of America. His sentence, which was described as the greatest miscarriage of justice, was quickly commuted, and he was declared persona non grata (unwelcome) and deported.

There is no doubt in my mind that many people (particularly the religious authorities) quaked after Marcus Garvey began to preach that the people of African descent in Europe and in the Western world are true descendants of the biblical Hebrew-Israelites—the descendants of the people who the prophet Moses brought out of Egyptian bondage.

Dr. Rudolph R. Windsor attested to that historical fact in *From Babylon to Timbuktu* (83–84). Although the dispersion of these Hebrew-Israelites who were living in the Holy Land began when the army of Antiochus IV (175–163 BC) invaded Palestine, it was intensified around AD 70 when the Romans obliterated their state, slaughtering an innumerable number of them. Many were sold as slaves, and hundreds of thousands fled into Africa. Dr. Windsor said, "The slave markets were full of black Jewish slaves" (*From Babylon to Timbuktu*, 84).

Both the Romans and Antiochus IV seemed to have had the same intention when they went into Palestine. Their aim was to destroy and remove all evidence of the existence of the black Hebrew-Israelites in the Holy Land.

In West Africa, they reestablished the ancient kingdom of Judah, which flourished up until the time they were brought into Egypt (bondage) again with slave ships.

Interestingly, the sixtieth question in the American citizenship quiz asked, "What group of people was taken to America and sold as slaves?" And the two answers given were: (a) Africans and (b) people from Africa. In the same way that the ancient Egyptians were oftentimes mistaken for the Hebrew-Israelites, in this time, it is difficult to distinguish between the Africans and the Hebrew-Israelites who were taken from Africa.

In Exodus, the daughters of Reuel, the priest of Midian, mistook Moses for an Egyptian (Exodus 2:19). He was not an Egyptian. In *100 Amazing Facts about the Negro*—with complete proof—J. A. Rogers agreed with Herodotus and Aristotle that the Ancient Egyptians were indeed black (17).

Both the Bible and the Koran (the sacred book of Islam) teach us that Moses was black, and most Bible scholars today who have accepted that fact still prefer to say he was a "man of color."

Moses was a Hebrew-Israelite, and the Bible classified them with the Ethiopians who are all black:

> Are you not as children of the Ethiopians unto me, O children of Israel? said the LORD [Jah]. (Amos 9:7 KJV)

> Put your hand into your bosom ... And when he took it out, his hand became as leprous as snow ... When he tucked it into his bosom for the second time, it regained the [dark] complexion of his other flesh. (Exodus 4:6–7 KJV)

Evidence of the kingdom of Judah in Africa can be seen on the map engraved by Emanuel Bowen (1694–1767) around 1747 when the transatlantic slave trade was in full swing. That map was made to direct our Colonial slavers to the kingdom of Judah in Negro Land, Africa, from which tens of millions of black Hebrew-Israelites were taken by force and brought to the so-called New World.

Yes, they were my ancestors, your ancestors, our black Hebrew-Israelite ancestors, who were ripped out of Africa, and brought here in the West where they worked as slaves for hundreds of years. Marcus Garvey taught that we, as a people, should look to Africa for the coming of our king and redeemer.

There is no doubt the many religious authorities found it very discomforting when he declared to the world that while we, the descendants of the biblical Hebrews, believe in the one and only God of creation, we were going to worship him through the spectacle of Ethiopia.

One must never forget that during the days of slavery, our ancestors were taught through the spectacle of our colonial slavers who believed that the Hebrew-Israelites, being black, were not human beings at all.

For hundreds of years, we were taught by our Christian slave masters that in order for us (the black Hebrew-Israelites) to be of any good, we had to become white as snow. That amounts to racism and religious bigotry

In biblical terms, the term "white as snow" meant to become leprous. And when one contracts leprosy, he was shunned by society. Therefore, as soon as our minds became leprous, they rejected us, and, just as they intended, we became the dregs of society.

The Bible said that Jah, our God, made us in his image and likeness. That clearly means that if one could have seen him, he would look like us. The Bible describes our God as having "hair like pure wool" (Daniel 7:9 KJV) and "feet like fine brass, as if they burned in fire" (Revelation 1:15 KJV). And that, my friend (before humankind knew racism), says that his hair is like that of the Negroes and that his skin is Ethiopic. Historical records show that before the dawn of racism, all the statues of the Virgin Mary and Christ thought the world were also black and Negroid. According to the *Washington Post* from May 4, 1979:

> Many of the Madonnas painted in earliest centuries
> of Christendom were black, according to historians,
> and it was not until the Renaissance that it became
> popular to give the Mother of Christ the features of
> a Florentine Maiden [a white woman].

The original paintings of Mary, mother of Eyesus (Jesus), showed that she had prominent black features. Now that we, the descendants of the black Hebrew-Israelites who survived the African Holocaust, know that our God is black, it is imperative that we worship him through the spectacle of Ethiopia.

Our Christian Colonial slavers looked upon the Negroes as inferior, the outcast of the races, the laughingstock of civilization, a people who must be made as white as snow. Garvey held that to be nothing short of racism and religious bigotry. Accordingly, he taught

43

that it is imperative that we put on the toga of race pride and put down the sort of ignominy that has prevented us from developing ourselves after so many centuries.

Now, during those years when Garvey was preparing the way and preaching the beatitude of bread and butter, Lidj Tafari grew, became strong in spirit, and was filled with wisdom. At the age of ten (unlike any other child that age in Ethiopia), he was writing, and he was fluent in the ancient Ge'ez as well as the modern Amharic language, which is still spoken in Ethiopia today.

In his autobiography, *My Life and Ethiopia's Progress*, he recalled that when he was about thirteen, the Father blessed him with spiritual and intellectual powers, which prepared him to lead all Ethiopians, at home and abroad.

His father was so impressed by the spirit that he saw in him that he conferred upon him (at age thirteen) the title, Dejazmatch (a military commander.) Even though he was not allowed to perform the duties that came with such noble post, he recalled that he was happy just to go into the office and sit down beside his father.

By that time, everybody in the court began to sense that he was no ordinary child. And that became obvious when, according to legend, an official in the court became so paralytic that he had to be helped out of Tafari's presence. Apparently, he became terrified and quaked after noticing the stigmata in the palm of Tafari's hands. The stigmata are the marks left by the nail wounds when Eyesus (Jesus) was crucified on the cross. It manifested itself again in 1966 when he visited Jamaica, and to that, Rita Marley (wife of Bob Marley) did bear witness publicly.

Tafari worked his way through the political order, obtaining the title of Ras, which commands more respect than the title of duke in other countries. Officially, he became known as Ras Tafari. He became governor of several provinces where he quickly effected needed administrative and tax reforms, all of which were welcomed by the working class. In 1917, he was proclaimed heir to the throne and regent with Queen Zauditu—who had just inherited the throne from her father, Menelik II—and he was crowned Negus (king) in 1928.

Thrust into a top leadership position, he immediately embarked on a plan aimed at the modernization of Ethiopia. The twentieth century had long dawned, and Ethiopia, to him, was still lagging in modern civilization. Moreover, the throne, the royal lineage, and the authority had become complacent; the Davidic monarchy was being degraded. It was time for the Lord to arise and raise up the fallen tabernacle of David.

Ethiopia's early rulers had, for too long, upheld a policy of international isolation, and now as regent, Ras Tafari believed that the time had come for the introduction of new foreign affairs policies that would help modernize Ethiopia. Cooperation with developed countries was a sure way to ensure that all Ethiopians would enjoy a higher standard of living.

Further, he quickly sought to make Ethiopian society more humane. It was common practice in Ethiopia to imprison someone who had defaulted on a loan. Also, public executions and the cutting off of limbs as forms of punishment were outlawed. He also proclaimed slavery to be illegal in that country. His aim was to modernize his medieval empire. He gave Ethiopia its first written constitution in 1931. Ethiopia was now stretching out its hands to God.

In 1922, he contacted Marcus Garvey through the UNIA (Universal Negro Improvement Association) in what (unfortunately) turned out to be a failed effort to encourage Africans/Ethiopians in the West to return to Ethiopia to help rebuild the ancient empire. Contrary to his opponent's remarks, Ras Tafari considered himself to be the leader of all people of African/Ethiopian descent.

To boost his new foreign policy, in 1923, he secured Ethiopia's membership in the League of Nations (the international body at the time which was the equivalent of today's UN).

Ethiopia shined among the constellation of nations when he toured Europe in 1924. He was warmly received at Buckingham Palace by King George. Rastafari oral tradition in Jamaica says that while he was at Buckingham Palace, the king put him to the test with an apple. King George could toss an apple into the air and cut it into twelve pieces with his sword before it fell to the ground. Ras Tafari proved himself by dividing an apple into thirteen pieces, one piece more than George. The twelve pieces (in Rastafari tradition) represent the twelve tribes of Israel, and the thirteenth piece, which, by the way, was stuck to the tip of his sword, meant that he could do much better than George and was also indicative of his lordship over the twelve tribes of Israel.

Although Ras Tafari never made mention of the apple incident in his autobiography, George was so impressed that at the end of his official visit, he returned to Tafari the crown of Emperor Theodore, which the British military had stolen from Ethiopia several years earlier.

On that same visit to London, vice chancellor of Cambridge University, Dr. Pearce—after reminding those present at a ceremony that Ras Tafari was a direct descendent of the biblical King Solomon of Jerusalem and the renowned queen of Sheba—conferred upon him the honorary degree of Doctor of Law. He also referred to him as having knowledge exceeding that of Orientals and Egyptians.

When he returned to Ethiopia, it became clear to many that the encouraging and strengthening of foreign relations was the right way forward. In fact, by that time, he had already concluded treaties of commerce and friendship with twelve foreign governments. He was now scouting for students to send to Europe and the United States to be trained as doctors and nurses, engineers, mechanics, aviators, scientists, and agriculturists. He saw education as the key that would enable him to exploit Ethiopia's human as well as its abundant natural resources.

Infrastructural development was also high on his priority list. It made way for the introduction of motor vehicles, airplanes, the telephone, schools of higher learning, hospitals, and the banking industry.

Ras Tafari ascended the throne on April 2, 1930, after the sudden death of Empress Zauditu. Then unheard of in the history of Ethiopia, he ordered that the coronation be postponed, giving foreign dignitaries sufficient time to make arrangements to attend the ceremony. He thought it would be good to invite to the coronation representatives of those foreign countries with whom Ethiopia had already established diplomatic relations. After all, this was no ordinary coronation, and the monarch was no ordinary man. Therefore, the world should be invited to witness his crowning.

Before coronation day, dignitaries had arrived from England, Italy, Belgium, Sweden, Japan, Egypt, France, the United States of America, Germany, Poland, and the Netherlands. There is no doubt in my mind that they all came with great expectations. They knew that Ras Tafari was going to be officially crowned king of Ethiopia. Moreover, they all knew that he was a direct descendant of the biblical King David and King Solomon of Jerusalem. Therefore, could this man be that promised seed of David who would restore the kingdom of Israel?

Then on the November 2, 1930—seven months after the passing of Empress Zauditu—the faithful people of Ethiopia, led by the archbishop, Abuna Qerillos, and graced by the presence of the foreign dignitaries, gathered at St. George's Cathedral for the official coronation. There, the archbishop, in accordance with the ancient biblical tradition, anointed H. I. M. (His Imperial Majesty) with the oil of kingship and placed the imperial crown (the royal diadem) upon his head, making him the 225th emperor to sit upon the throne of David.

What is amazing and comforting is that it was the same throne—the throne of the kingdom of the Lord, Jah, over Israel—that King Solomon occupied about twenty-eight hundred years prior.

Throne, as used in biblical sense, goes far beyond the seat or chair occupied by a king or queen. It actually connotes royal lineage and authority, and it is that royal lineage and authority that Jahweh had promised David that he would establish forever. The kingdom of David has always been taken to be a literal earthly kingdom and not some spiritual realm or pie-in the-sky idea that you cannot inherit until the day you die.

At the coronation, his new name (the same name which, while he was still a youth, he claimed that nobody knew) along with his biblical titles of honor were finally revealed. The world had just witnessed the coronation of Haile Selassie I, elect of God, Jah (the Father), Emperor of Ethiopia, King of kings and Lord of lords; conquering Lion of the tribe of Judah, and Root of David.

The name Haile Selassie literally means power/might of the Holy Trinity. As power of the Holy Trinity, His Imperial Majesty asserted his place in the Godhead. Haile Selassie had just declared to the whole world that he and God, Jah (the Father), are one. And, truly, that is what earned him the name Jah Rastafari. Emperor Haile Selassie I, Jah Rastafari, was the one in whom all the fullness of the Godhead was pleased to indwell for the second time.

The scripture teaches that our God, Jah, exists in three persons, and that is how the doctrine of the Holy Trinity was founded. The Godhead is made up of Jah, the Father, Jah, the Son, and Jah, the Holy Spirit.

When the Father was ready to create man, he said, "Let us make man in our image, after our likeness" (Genesis 1:26 KJV).

One can observe the Trinity in action in the book of Genesis, during the creation of the universe as well as in Matthew, when Eyesus was baptized by John the Baptist. Yes, he too, went down by the River Jordan to experience John's baptism for the remission of sins.

Let us look at the example given in verses 16–17 of the third chapter of the book of Matthew (KJV). There we see Eyesus, the Son, being baptized by John, and as soon as he came out of the water, the Spirit descended upon him in the form of a dove, and then the audible voice of the Father said, "This is my beloved Son."

Today, the Rasta man exalts Haile Selassie as Jah Rastafari, the Son incarnate for the second time. When he first came to the earth in the personality of Eyesus, he did not come in his kingly character; instead, he came as the lamb to the slaughter.

Caiaphas, the high priest at the temple in Jerusalem, said, "It was expedient that one man should die for the people" (John 18:14 KJV). And that is why this author also believe that Eyesus Kristos (Jesus Christ) was the one who went to the cross.

Eyesus shunned the idea of being crowned king. Immediately after he fed the multitude of people with five barley loaves and two fishes, the people wanted to make him their king.

Matthew 14:21 (KJV) puts the number of people at about "five thousand men, besides women and children." Therefore, there could have easily been about twelve thousand people there. Eyesus fed twelve thousand people with only five loaves and two fishes, and after everyone had their fill, his disciples collected enough leftovers to fill twelve baskets, which stunned the crowd: "This is, of a truth, that prophet that should come into the world" (John 6:14 KJV).

Having accepted that as truth as evidence of prophecy being fulfilled right before their eyes, they conspired to "take him by force, to make him a (their) king" (John 6:15 KJV). Then, Eyesus, knowing it was not the will of the Father, fled into the mountains. That is the 100 percent proof that Eyesus did not come into this world (at his first advent) to govern the children of Israel. That was not the will of our Father. Again, he came as the lamb to the slaughter.

Eyesus was never crowned king. The so-called crown of thorns with which the heathens mocked him should never be regarded as the crowning of a king. Before the foundations of the earth were laid, Jahweh had plans in place for the crowning of the Righteous Branch of David, whom he had intended to raise up for the second time. Ras Tafari came, and was crowned, not only as king, but as King of kings, declaring to the world that the Lord had not forgotten his promise to his servant, David.

Although hundreds of direct descendants of David had sat upon the throne, Haile Selassie outshined them all by being the promised Righteous Branch. He governed by divine right. The laws of the kings of Ethiopia states that only the male line of the descendants had the right of succession to the throne. The oath that the nobles and governors of Ethiopia took after Makeda abdicated and made her son king claimed that "no one except the male seed of David, the son of Solomon … shall ever reign over Ethiopia" (*Kebra Nagast*, 147).

The conquering Lion of the tribe of Judah brought hope to the tottering Davidic monarchy. Throughout his reign, he taught that much of the impending calamities that shall befall humankind can be averted if we embrace international and interracial amity. The dream of lasting peace, world citizenship, and the rule of international morality is attainable—and it need not remain but a fleeting illusion to be pursued.

Whenever he would lament on the ills of modern civilization, he would, with the same breath, offer the simple and practical solutions whereby humankind can realize justice and peace. Haile Selassie made it abundantly clear that there can never be—on the part of any person or nation—a legitimate reason or interest to justify war. If all nations were to choose not to go to war with each other, the peace and security they all crave could be realized.

Within days of his coronation, Marcus Garvey—on the behalf of all people of African descent living in the West—sent His Imperial Majesty a telegram, wishing him a "peaceful, prosperous, and progressive reign."

Garvey then reaffirmed that H. I. M. was ready to receive anyone from the West who was willing to go and settle in his kingdom. He implored us to hold up the hands of our emperor.

That excerpt reminds me of the conflict between Israel and Amalek (Exodus 17:8–13 KJV). In the same way that Aaron and Hur had to hold up the hands of Moses to guarantee success in battle, so all Ethiopians—all people of African descent at home and abroad— were supposed to work with Selassie to rebuild the tottering kingdom of David. Without our support, the emperor would not succeed. His success guaranteed our success as well.

Unfortunately, Garvey's call went unheeded. In fact, whether it was for financial or geographical reasons, not even Garvey himself heeded the call. Instead, he chose to open negotiations with the president of Liberia to set up a colony there. Consequently, negotiations broke down, and the Liberian government took back the lands promised to Garvey—and all efforts to return to Ethiopia were suspended.

The Messiah did make his Second Advent in the personality of Emperor Haile Selassie I of Ethiopia. However, because most people expected him to come down from the clouds with brilliant display, his coming almost went unnoticed. Again, he "was in the world [the second time] and the world knew him not" (John 1:10 KJV).

In the same way that the prophet Elijah returned in the person of John the Baptist, so did the Messiah in the person of His Imperial Majesty, Haile Selassie I.

Reputed author J. A. Rogers was present at his coronation as a correspondent for the *Amsterdam News*, and he had the privilege to engage Haile Selassie in conversation on numerous occasions. In fact, on one occasion, His Majesty was the one who summoned Rogers to his court. Rogers remarked that after observing the King of kings and speaking with him for hours, he also felt that Selassie was like a black edition of the pictured Christ.

Despite his seeming intention to ridicule and discredit Haile Selassie, one of his critics was nevertheless convinced that Selassie never appeared to have any common negative human emotions. He also agreed that nobody ever reported him uttering any harsh or angry words. In short, Selassie's critic bore witness of his godhood. And it has always been regarded as good when others, especially those who hate without cause, bear true witness of another.

That reminds me of Balaam, the false prophet who set out to curse the Hebrew children as they journeyed toward the Promised Land. However, instead of cursing, Jah caused him to "bless them instead" (see Numbers 22–24 KJV). He discovered that no man can curse anyone who Jah does not curse or defy anyone who Jah has not defied.

An English man who frequented Selassie's home while he was in exile in Bath, England, testified that whenever he was in the presence of Haile Selassie, he always felt like he was in the presence of somebody who was more than man. And we must not forget that that is the very same way that our renowned Jewish historian, Josephus, felt about him when he made his first advent in the personality of Eyesus Kristos.

The Pharisees believed that if someone were to bear witness of themselves, then whatever good they may say would not be true. When they confronted Eyesus because they thought he bore witness of himself, he said, "Even though I bear witness of myself, my witness is true … I am one that bear witness of myself" (John 8:14, 18 KJV). And like Eyesus, Haile Selassie, who purposed in his heart to behave himself wisely in a perfect way and to walk within his house with a perfect heart is also one who did bear true witness of himself.

This author also bears witness that His Imperial Majesty is the returned Messiah, and through the power of the Holy Spirit, he continues to reconcile the world to himself. Remember that no man can come to Ras Tafari, except the Father—who sent him—draws them.

Regrettably, a lot of people have not yet accepted Haile Selassie as the returned King of kings and Lord of lords due to ignorance. They have never open-mindedly taken the time to get to know more about him besides what they may have heard in a song. I admonish everyone to get to know His Imperial Majesty. Nobody can shake the truth from its place, and the truth is that Haile Selassie I did declare to the world through his very name that he was that Elect of God, Jah the Father, Emperor of Ethiopia, King of all kings, Lord of all lords, Conquering Lion of the tribe of Judah, and Root of David, according to the flesh.

Again, Christ had his Second Advent in the personality of Haile Selassie I of Ethiopia. And for the second time, he "came unto his own and his own received him not" (John 1:11 KJV).

One of the primary reasons Eyesus Kristos was rejected at his first advent was because he did not meet the expectations of the people, especially the fanatical religious leaders. They expected him to come in pomp and glory, and because he was born in a manger, they rejected him as their Messiah. In fact, at one time, not even his own paternal brothers—James, Simon, Joseph, and Judas—believed he was the Anointed One (John 7:5 KJV, Matthew 13:55 KJV). Their denial took place so that the prophetic words of David, as written in the book of Psalms, could be fulfilled:

> I have become a stranger unto my brethren, and an
> alien unto my mother's children. (Psalm 69:8 KJV)

Eyesus Kristos was also rejected at his first advent because he did not encourage the toppling of the political establishment and proclaim himself leader or king.

Philip told Nathanael that they had found Eyesus of Nazareth, and he was the one "of whom Moses in the law, and the prophets, did write" (John 1:45 KJV). He said, "Can any good thing come out of Nazareth?" (John 1:46 KJV). Fortunately, the Father drew him, and he eventually accepted him as the Son of God, Jah:

> Thou art the Son of God [Jah], thou art the King of
> Israel. (John 1:49 KJV)

Similarly, many people today have refused to accept Ras Tafari as the returned Christ simply because he is Ethiopian. And, like Nathaniel, they say, can any good thing come out of Africa?

Again, no man can come to Ras Tafari, except the Father, who had sent him, draw him.

There remains nothing that the Rasta man can do or say that will convince anybody that Haile Selassie I is the returned Messiah. Only the spirit of the Highest can do that. One must remember that the Rasta man "did pipe and you did not dance; he mourned and you have not wept" (Luke 7:32 KJV). Selah.

Chapter 3

The Temptation of Haile Selassie

There hath no temptation taken you, but such as
is common to man ... God [Jah] will not permit
you to be tempted above that you are able: but
will with the temptation ... make way to escape.
—1 Corinthians 10:13 (KJV)

THE WORD *TEMPTATION* has its origin in several ancient Hebrew and Greek words, which all seem to suggest "trial," "to prove," "to examine" and "to put to the test."

Temptation builds character, and it helps recreate godlikeness within humanity. While being tested, potential victims must prove themselves worthy of their "calling" in this life. On the other hand, temptation can also be regarded as an enticement to wrongdoing and a luring with the promise of reward—whether it be pleasure, power, or material gain. Consequently, if the potential victim succumbs, the tempter would have caused his victim to stray from the course they should have rightly taken.

Equally important, temptation must never be construed as evil or sinful. Trials are a part of the divine plan for everybody's life. What is important is the way in which the person being tested responds to the temptation. Yes, one's response to temptation determines whether they or the tempter gets the victory.

The potential victim has a choice in the matter and, therefore, needs not succumb or yield to the subtle demands or wishes of the tempter. The one who falls victim when put to the test is often weak-willed and inclined to believe their tempter. Also, their response is usually one of quickly resisting and then slowly giving way to the temptation.

In any event, whether the victim thwarts the tempter or succumbs, their response says something about their personality and character. Let us take the temptation of Adam and Eve as an example. It was a simple test of obedience to the Creator. When the tempter confronted Eve about eating of the tree in the middle of the garden, she held fast that neither she nor her husband, Adam, were permitted to eat therefrom. She even remarked—unlike what was written in the scripture—that they were not even allowed to "touch it" (Genesis 3:3 KJV). Seemingly, she had no intention of doing so. Her tempter told her otherwise. When he persisted, she succumbed—first by resisting and then gradually by yielding.

Eve proved herself to be an unreserved person who often leaped before she looked, and that makes one wonder if that is the reason the tempter chose not to tempt her husband instead. The tempter may have targeted the weaker vessel. She eventually deceived her husband, thereby plunging humanity into original sin.

Today, we refer to Adam and Eve's yield to the appeal of the devil as the fall:

> By one man, sin entered into the world, and death by sin, and so death passed upon all men. (Romans 5:12 KJV)

From the general tone of scripture, one gets the impression that Eyesus Kristos (Jesus Christ) was the "next" or "second Adam." In fact, 1 Corinthians 15:45 (KJV) went even further by calling him the "last Adam."

The first Adam brought sin and death into the world, and the second came to take away sin and death. Unlike the first Adam and his wife, the second, when tempted, did not resist and then succumb; he resisted the tempter without wavering.

Remember, the divine plan for Eyesus was for him to offer himself up as the "one-time" sacrifice for sin. It was crucial for him to remain unblemished and spotless, and to prove that, he had to undergo severe testing. If he sinned and failed, he would no longer be worthy of that high calling.

The Spirit lead him into the wilderness to be tested by the devil (Luke 4:1–13), but the actual trial did not even begin until after forty days and forty nights had passed. Since he was fasting, he was so much in tune with Jah, the Father, that the wicked one could not get through to him. Therefore, the tempter seemed to have waited until he was hungry and physically weak before he attacked. He tried in vain to make him display self-conceitedness, to make him "show off," as it were, the powers that he possesses, which should be used only to bring glory to the name of Jah, the Father. He was hungry, but he did not need to prove anything to the evil one by turning stone into bread. He did not need to jump from the pinnacle of the temple to prove that he was the Son of God. He clearly knew who he was and what he was capable of doing.

The tempter also tried to get him to worship falsely with the promise of power and authority. He wanted Eyesus to serve him instead of Jah, the Father. Ultimately, the tempter wanted him to question and betray his trust and dependence upon Jah. Eyesus prevailed, fulfilled his mission, and returned to the Father. Who knows what would have become of humankind if he had succumbed?

Eyesus (Jesus) made his Second Advent in July 1892, the year of John the Apostle. He returned to this earth in like manner as his followers had seen him go the first time. He departed in the flesh, returned in the flesh, and was born of a woman.

On November 2, 1930, at St. George's Cathedral in Ethiopia, the archbishop, Abuna Qerillos, anointed him with the oil of kingship and proclaimed him Haile Selassie I, elect of God, Jah, the Father;

King of kings, and Lord of lords; Conquering Lion of the tribe of Judah, and Root of David, according to the flesh.

Haile Selassie means power/might of the Holy Trinity, and his mission was to rebuild the tottering kingdom of David, which essentially represents the kingdom of heaven upon this earth. He had to prove himself worthy of that high calling again. His faith and obedience to Jah, the Father, had to be put to the test again. As sovereign of the oldest empire in the world, he must demonstrate his commitment and loyalty and affirm his divine right of kingship.

When it comes to the issue of ancient lineages in the world, there is none that is older than the Ethiopian royal family. According to *National Geographic*, June 1931:

> The Ethiopians list of their kings, dates as far back from Ori of 4478 BC to Haile Selassie I of AD 1930.

When Selassie was physically present with us, he traced and named his ancestors to King Solomon of Jerusalem and Makeda, the queen of Sheba. J. A. Rogers compared it with that of King George VI of England and said that it could be older by as much as 6,130 years (*100 Amazing Facts about the Negro*, 12).

Haile Selassie's time of severe testing began shortly after his coronation and lasted until the very day that his kingdom suffered violence. In a blatant act of provocation, the Italian government intensified its efforts to take Ethiopia from His Imperial Majesty, earth's rightful ruler. The latecomer in the "scramble for Africa," without notice, began to occupy vast amounts of Ethiopian lands under the pretext that Ethiopia had no well-defined borders.

Mussolini pretended to have forgotten that the Italian delegate (Count Bonin Longare) made it clear to the League of Nations in 1923 that Ethiopia did have clearly defined borders. Apparently, it was a requirement of the League of Nations—of which Ethiopia was already a member—that any country seeking membership in its general assembly must have well-defined borders. And Mussolini knew that since he had been instrumental in helping Ethiopia gain its membership in the League of Nations.

After Selassie reaffirmed that his country did have well-defined borders, they offered to pay him millions of liras (the Italian currency) for the parcels of land they so badly craved. As it turned out, they were quite cunningly offering to "buy out" Ethiopia, a little piece at a time.

His Majesty rejected the offer because he felt that the Italian government was actually tempting him to do what they knew he would not do. He held fast to his identity and integrity and did not give the inheritance of his ancestors to the wicked and the deceitful.

Outwitted and ashamed that Selassie had rejected his offer, Benito Mussolini resorted to wage war against the righteous seed of David. And as might be expected, Pope Pius XI came to Mussolini's assistance. Yes, the Italian government set itself, and the papacy took council together against the His Imperial Majesty. The pope bestowed his full blessing upon Mussolini, ordering his soldiers to undertake a civilization mission, a Christian reconquest of the world. Conveniently, they were to begin with Ethiopia, the land of the Conquering Lion of the tribe of Judah.

In *The Great Popes through History* (492), it is written that as soon as Pope Pius XI (whose pontificate lasted from 1922–39) took office, he flirted with the idea of a "Christian re-conquest of the world." He believed that humanity had lost all sense of "spiritual authority and belief in a higher power." Therefore, he quickly charged the Catholic Church with the task of restoring spiritual belief and the promotion of the kingship of Christ.

Also, like Pope Gregory VII (1073–1085), who laid the ground works for crusading, and Pope Urban II (1088–99), who proclaimed the first official Crusade in 1095, Pope Pius XI had fallen in love with the notion that military ventures were a sure way for the Catholic Church to ensure that it would meet the spiritual needs of its members and assert its political leadership in Europe. Pius had concluded negotiations with the Italian government in February of

1929, which, besides making Catholicism the state religion, resulted in the establishment of the sovereign state of Vatican City.

Now he knew that the opportune time had presented itself for the papacy to embark on its so-called Christian reconquest of the world. All he had to contribute was his full papal blessings since Mussolini already had the so-called Roman Christian soldiers ready and waiting to shed innocent blood.

Pope Pius XI truly believed that warfare in the service of the church was not sinful at all. As long as you can say that it was in the service of the church, it became an acceptable form of violence. He also upheld the notion that since God himself instituted holy warfare, crusading was not evil.

The pope, supposing himself to be God's first vicar on earth—someone whose highest goal was the unification of humanity under the scepter of Christ—availed himself to the service of the devil. Those two emissaries of Satan—Mussolini and Pope Pius XI—took council against the Ethiopians soon after the archbishop of St. George's Cathedral announced the kingship of Haile Selassie I. That bold declaration frightened Vatican City, and that strong feeling of indignation that kindled within the pope's heart overshadowed the peace of Christ.

Who was this Ethiopian king who was proclaiming himself to be the power and might of the Holy Trinity? Did Christ return in that person without telling the pope? For that cause, Rome thirsted after his blood. Therefore, Pius reinstituted crusading in 1935. Yes, he declared a so-called holy war on Ethiopians.

One must never forget the eight major Crusades that took place in Europe between 1095 and 1270 were all military expeditions, and they were all commissioned by popes who thought they were for a "holy cause." And to Pius, a Christian reconquest of the world, beginning with Ethiopia, meant just that.

The forces of evil—Mussolini and his military—indiscriminately rained down bombs and poisoned gas upon soldiers and civilians alike. They spared not even the lives of the old men, women, or children. Even the animals grazing in the pastures met the same fate.

Those Roman Christian soldiers, after ransacking the church buildings, would ring the bell as if to summon the faithful people to worship. Then they would shut the doors—with the worshippers inside—and set the buildings on fire.

Nobody would have expected such cruelty from a so-called Christian nation, but that's exactly what Pope Pius XI meant when he thought of his Christian reconquest of the world—and that is what Mussolini meant by embarking on a civilizing mission.

The devout Ethiopians who survived the massacre believed they literally had endured a fight with the devil himself. When the massacre was over, an estimated 750,000 innocent people had lost their lives. In *The Ethiopian Tewahedo Church*, Archbishop Yesehaq provided pictures of Roman soldiers posing with the severed head of an Ethiopian in their hands. During the ruination, they washed the earth with blood.

Even before the war was over, Mussolini hastily declared to the world that Haile Selassie had abdicated his throne and given full control of Ethiopia to Italy. He even proclaimed Victor Emmanuel III (the king of Italy) to be the new king of Ethiopia. As might be expected, the European nations sided with Italy. Apparently, that is what they truly wanted to see. Italy must get a slice of the cake too.

The only five members of the League of Nations that refused to recognize Italy's illicit claim over Ethiopia were the United States, Mexico, China, New Zealand, and the Soviet Union.

Had His Imperial Majesty truly abdicated and secretly sold Ethiopia to the Italians? The world needs to know and know quickly—and that responsibility lies with none other than the rightful ruler of Ethiopia, Haile Selassie I. That meant that he must go to Geneva, in the European wilderness, to address the League of Nations. If he stayed in Ethiopia and continued to fight alongside his soldiers, he might get killed—and then who would plead Ethiopia's case before the world and before the League of Nations? If he did not appear before the League of Nations, his absence, in no uncertain terms, will be construed to mean that he was no longer the king of Ethiopia, and Italy's claim over Ethiopia would be upheld.

Since the war was far from over—and all means of communicating with the outside world had virtually been cut off—how would he receive timely notice of his meetings with the General Assembly? Staying in Ethiopia was definitely not an option, and His Imperial Majesty left for Europe. While there, he sojourned in Bath, England.

Within days of his first scheduled appearance before the General Assembly, the devil, acting through some of his very own trusted advisers, told him to abandon his plans to go to Geneva. They thought it was prudent to dispatch a delegation instead. In obedience to the voice of the Spirit of Truth, Ethiopia's rightful ruler rejected their advice; the matter was too crucial to be entrusted to envoys. The tempter's aim had been to prevent His Imperial Majesty from appearing in person before the League of Nations.

Firmly resolved, the Lion roared. He must go to Geneva to let the League of Nations know what had taken place in his country. He considered going to Geneva as the rightful leader of Ethiopia to be his highest duty.

As the Conquering Lion roared before the General Assembly, Mussolini, the devil's advocate, sensing the agony of defeat, squawked that the League of Nations should not permit a vanquished country to have envoys in the General Assembly. Now, one can see why Selassie insisted that the matter was too crucial for envoys to handle.

Mussolini treated His Majesty as a mere representative of Ethiopia and not as its rightful leader. Had he sent a delegation to Geneva, Mussolini—because he had the backing of the European nations—would have had them expelled from the meeting.

Standing firm, Haile Selassie made it clear that he was present there in the capacity of emperor of Ethiopia, and that thwarted Mussolini's plot. The Conquering Lion of the tribe of Judah prevailed.

Unable to defeat the Conquering Lion, Mussolini hatched a plot aimed at having Ethiopia expelled from the League of Nations. He must have been a man devoid of the faculty of logical thought. The leader of the aggressor nation was demanding that the League of Nations expel from its General Assembly the nation against whom an aggression had been committed. He argued that since he had virtually dismantled its government, Ethiopia, as a sovereign authority, did not exist and did not belong in the General Assembly. If Ethiopia were to lose its membership seat in the General Assembly, Italy's claim over her could become legitimized. That was how badly the Italians wanted that part of our country.

Italy had been instrumental in having Ethiopia admitted to the League of Nations, and now Mussolini was asking for its dismissal simply because His Majesty would not bow down and worship him. The King of kings will not do and cannot do the biddings of the enemy of the throne of David.

Mussolini knew he had violated the covenant of the League of Nations when he invaded Ethiopia. Therefore, it was Italy, not Ethiopia, that was at risk of being expelled from the League of Nations.

According to Article 16, subsection 4, of the covenant:

> Any member of the League which has violated any Covenant of the League may be declared to be no longer a member of the League by a vote of the council concurred in by the representatives of all the other members of the League represented thereon.

Mussolini bullied the General Assembly into making Selassie prove whether there was still a functional government in Ethiopia that was run by Ethiopians instead of focusing on the issue of Italy's unprovoked invasion, but the Conquering Lion of Judah would not be caught in that snare. He presented the committee with written correspondence from his prime minister, Bitwoded Wolde Tsadik, and other government officials as proof that Ethiopia still had an Ethiopian-controlled government. Further, he made it clear that because of Italian invasion, he had ordered that the operations of government be moved from Addis Ababa (the capital city) to the province of Gore.

Ethiopia's rightful ruler was vindicated, and the General Assembly decided that Ethiopia should retain its membership seat. It would have been by divine intervention that most of the countries that did openly recognize Italy's claim over Ethiopia voted in its favor. In fact, thirty- nine nations of the forty-nine represented sided with Ethiopia.

The Conquering Lion had prevailed. He denounced those who sided with Italy and humbly boasted that Ethiopia's seat in the General Assembly was irrevocable. While he was awaiting the fulfillment of his mission in the European wilderness, the Lion of Judah made his den in Bath, England. Within a short time, he became financially hungry. He was on the verge of bankruptcy.

The Lion was so hungry that he filed a lawsuit against a telecommunications company to access monies he had invested with them. It turned out that that move only worsened his financial crisis. The court did not rule in his favor, and as might be expected, he was ordered to cover the court's fees. I believe the court's decision was influenced by Italy's claim over Ethiopia since England was one of the European nations that recognized Italy's illegal occupation of Ethiopia. As far as the court was concerned, Haile Selassie, as claimant, could not be exonerated by an English court.

As might be expected, the tempter quickly offered bread in the form of some viable financial offers. This time, he did not ask that he turn stones into bread to slake his hunger; he was now much sleeker and was going to provide the bread.

A British film production company offered to quench his financial thirst if he would play a leading role in *Flight by Night*. His Majesty was being tested for self-conceitedness, self-interest, and self-esteem. Without wavering, he refused to partake or indulge himself in any activities that could cause him to stray from his charted course. He was on a mission to seek justice for the people of Ethiopia and would not be sidetracked.

Did the film producers have any good intentions when they tried to lure the Lion into taking part in the film? After considering the circumstances that led Selassie into the European wilderness in the first place, I believe the very name of the film suggested mockery and was designed to ridicule him. The Lion refused, and the tempter's plot was foiled again.

The next temptation came when the Texas Centennial Exhibition offered him up to $150,000 to take part in a show. Certainly, that amount of money at that time would have helped slake his financial thirst in a big way. The tempter sought to dishonor the King of kings by testing his character, his integrity, and his commitment to the Ethiopian cause. Get him involved in anything other than the people's business, and the whole world would see a greedy, selfish, and untrustworthy leader immersing himself in worldly pleasure while his subjects were suffering at home.

The King of kings in an exhibition show? His Majesty was neither clown nor jester, and they wanted to make him the star of their show. Although he might have been low on cash, he was not greedy for money. I am of the opinion that they likened that sum of money which they were offering His Majesty to the thirty pieces of silver Judas took to betray Eyesus Kristos (Jesus the Christ). Firmly resolved, he rejected the offer, demonstrating that as a man of integrity, filled with dignity, no amount of silver could buy him.

Convinced that a drowning man will always catch at a straw, Mussolini, in an act of desperation, made His Majesty another offer, which he thought was irresistible. The offer was supposed to bring an end to his financial predicament. He challenged the Lord of lords to pick a country that he liked—anywhere in the world—and he would buy him a palace in that country. Besides, he would also get one million guineas in spending money.

Should the hungry Lion fall for that overly generous offer, he and his family could "live happily ever after." A guinea was a gold coin that was minted by the British government, and each coin was worth twenty-one shillings. The tempter was dangling one million guineas over the head of the King of kings.

The tempter, at that point, tried to snare His Majesty by making him promises. When the devil thought that Eyesus was not yielding to temptation, he made him promises:

All these things will I give thee. (Matthew 4:9 KJV)

Mussolini was trying that same tactic on Haile Selassie. A hungry lion is bound to rip apart easy prey.

Like his ancestor, Solomon, Selassie knew that "money answereth all things" (Ecclesiastes 10:19 KJV), and that "money is a defense" (Ecclesiastes 7:12 KJV). Therefore, he need not depend on the fundraising efforts of the Abyssinia Society for sustenance. Accept the offer, and "all will be well." Oh, what sweet temptation!

Again, the tempter tried to lure the Lion into selling Ethiopia. Also, his intention was to prevent him from returning to his country. By keeping him out, the Italians could move in fully and occupy Ethiopia. In fact, he made it abundantly clear that if His Majesty was willing to accept his seemingly irresistible offer, he was also required to renounce his kingship. He would have to abdicate his throne. In addition, he would have had to sign a document telling the world—in writing—that he had sold Ethiopia to the Italians.

As if he knew beforehand that the tempter was going to bring up the issue of his kingship, Selassie had announced before he left for Europe that he was never going to abdicate his throne or abandon his coronation name. What made Mussolini think he could actually buy His Majesty's royal lineage and authority?

In the book of Acts, Simon offered the apostles Peter and John money if they would give him the power to impart the Holy Spirit to others (Acts 8:17–19 KJV).

His Majesty rebuked the tempter sharply, leaving no question about his resolve to protect and preserve the oldest empire in the world. And to Mussolini—and anyone else who thought they could trick him into selling Ethiopia since they couldn't get it by fighting war—he made it abundantly clear that he had left his country with one intention in mind, and that was to seek justice for his people in Ethiopia. Ethiopia was not up for sale.

In what seemed to have been a move to allow him time to reconsider the offer, the tempter left him for a while. After one year, he returned with another wishy-washy offer, beseeching His Majesty to betray Ethiopian trust. He spoke as though Ethiopia actually belonged to the Italians. Along with one million pounds, he was now willing to share Ethiopia with Selassie. By 1938, the League of Nations had not yet ruled on whether Ethiopia belonged to Italy or the Ethiopians. Therefore, if he could get Selassie to accept that offer, it would become clear that Italy was truly in control of Ethiopia.

As might be expected, His Majesty resisted sharply, making clear that the issue regarding his country was not about his personal well-being. It was about the people of Ethiopia and territorial integrity. The only issue that was open for discussion was the securing of justice (not from Italy, but from the League of Nations) for Ethiopians.

Haile Selassie foiled the devil's plot to make him abdicate the throne of David and take Ethiopia away from the Ethiopians. He would not be deceived by Rome. He would not sell, give away, or slice up Ethiopia like a cake. Emperor Haile Selassie knew that giving up the inheritance of his fathers was forbidden, and he proved himself worthy of his high calling. He demonstrated integrity, honesty, and selflessness—qualities that neither Mussolini nor Pope Pius possessed. Moreover, he demonstrated to the world that he was godlike. The Conquering Lion of the tribe of Judah prevailed.

As fate would have it, the balance of power in Europe quickly shifted, and England and France stepped up their policing efforts in the Mediterranean, which made Italy afraid that her access to the Suez Canal was being jeopardized. Also, Germany had begun its occupation of several European countries. After Hitler turned his attention on France, Mussolini quickly joined forces with him and declared war on France and England, which was exactly what Haile Selassie had foreseen several months prior.

Italy's alliance with Hitler became its self-imposed death sentence. The Lion was so confident that Italy would fall that—ten months earlier—he had sent an agent to Ethiopia to gather intelligence in preparation for his return. It was clear that the time had come for him to get out of the European wilderness.

He left on the night of June 25, 1940, and after many days of negotiations, the British armed forces helped him reinstate his sovereignty in Ethiopia.

Haile Selassie was tested, and he did not succumb. He proved himself faithful and true to the people of Ethiopia and the house of David. He passed through the fire and came out as pure gold.

The Conquering Lion of Judah had prevailed. Selah.

Chapter 4

A Token of Salvation

MOST PEOPLE TODAY accept the written accounts (particularly the biblical account) that say our first parents, Adam and Eve, made a poor choice against our Creator, which resulted in the so-called fall of humankind. The fall, in turn, lends itself to the concept of original sin, which carried the penalty of death—both physically and spiritually.

Spiritual death is a breakdown—or the end of—fellowship between Creator and creature. It is the separation from the Lord, Jah. The spiritual genetic material passed on to us by our first parents was contaminated with sin. Genetic fingerprinting revealed that all humanity was fated to sin and its attendant consequences.

On the other hand, physical death is the end of physical or biological life as we know it. When physical death occurs, we often say that the person has "passed on," "passed away," "deceased," or "no longer alive." After that, we put them "six feet under." In support of this, the biblical account says that "sin entered the world, and death by sin, and so death passed upon all men" (Romans 5:12 KJV).

The fall left humanity in desperate need of some urgent spiritual genetic engineering. To survive or to be free from original sin and its consequences, humankind had to be reconciled to their Creator, Jah.

Before we address the subject of salvation, we must take a much closer look at the fall through the spectacle of the Bible. The Bible is the only book that contains the most basic set of instructions a person should acquire before they leave the earth. "B" is for basic; "I" is for instructions; "B" is for before, "L" is for leaving, and "E" stands for earth. The Bible is our basic instructions before leaving earth!

By now, most people would have embraced the biblical account of creation. We did not evolve as some skeptics would have us believe. We were created in the image and likeness of Jah, the unchanging God of creation.

For the most part, an image can be defined as a molded, carved, painted, or even pictured representation of a god, person, animal, or thing. The term *likeness* seems to connote a "semblance," "copy," or "portrait" of a god, person, animal, or thing. The two terms are interlaced, and they both suggest similarity in appearance or form. An image, whether carved, molded, or painted, would have the outward appearance of the person or thing its sculptor or painter purposed to replicate. That resemblance renders it a representation of the person or thing that its maker had in mind.

An idol—even though its maker might have given it humanoid features—would remain a lifeless and nonfunctional object. Although it may look like a human being, the image of a human being does not possess human qualities. Until somebody destroys it or until it decays, it shall remain lifeless and nondescript:

> And God, [Jah], said, let us make man in our image, after our likeness. (Genesis 1:26 KJV)

Of all the living creatures that were created, only humans—male and female—were created with the "image" or "likeness" of the Highest. Humans were created after Jahweh's kind, and all other creatures were created after their own kind:

> And God, [Jah], made the beast of the earth after its kind, and the cattle after their kind, and everything that creeps ... after its kind. (Genesis 1:25 KJV)

Humankind, therefore, is the living image of the living God, Jah. We were endowed at creation with godlike qualities and personality traits. The other living creatures were infused with instincts.

Our God, Jah, is a triune God. The Godhead is made up of the Father, the Son, and the Holy Spirit. We refer to the three-in-one unity as the Holy Trinity: one God existing in three distinct personalities.

Jah is Spirit and only becomes visible when he wills to manifest himself to us. Such manifestations are often in the forms of human beings. For example, when Eyesus first came to earth, he came in the form of a human being. His apostle John attested to that fact in his writing (John 5:18; 10:33 KJV). On those two occasions, Eyesus subtly declared that he was equal with God, Jah, the Father. As might be expected, his remarks displeased the teachers of the Jews. They simply could not overstand how Eyesus (Jesus), "being a man, maketh himself God" (John 5:18 KJV).

Likewise, when Haile Selassie came to the earth, he too was God, Jah, who manifested himself in the flesh. The Rasta man refers to Selassie as Jah Rastafari because we overstand that Ras Tafari and the Father are one: the Father in him and him in the Father.

These manifestations are different from that of the humanoid beings we often call angels. When Jah sends a messenger (an angel) on an earthly mission, they also take on the likeness of a human being, but they must never be taken to be God on earth.

Like his Creator, humans are also tripartite or three-in-one beings. A human has a body, a soul (mind), and a spirit. A person's spirit is invisible. It is the epicenter of intellect, character, and emotions. If a person could see their own spirit, it would look the same way that they look physically. That is why John, in his vision of the anointed one, could have described he who is a spirit as having the physical appearance of a human being (Revelation 1:13–18 KJV).

The soul is inseparably tied to the spirit; it is like the essence of being, the inner self, the inherent part of us that alludes to self-awareness or consciousness. The scripture says that after Jahweh breathed the breath of life into man's nostrils, man "became a living soul" (Genesis 2:7 KJV).

Our spirits manifest themselves in our physical bodies; therefore, we "appear." Our bodies "house" our spirits. Like our Creator, we are also personal and moral beings. We are capable of consciously making right or wrong decisions and are free to act accordingly. These are the basic, unique elements of personality that separates us from all other living creatures. These attributes make us the living functional image of the living God, Jah. Through these character traits, we have become godlike.

When looked at from a secular standpoint, the image-likeness concept becomes less complex. How often do we hear the expression "spitting image" when referring to someone's offspring? We say that boy or girl is the spitting image of their father or mother. One of the most intriguing accounts about a child being in the image and likeness of its father can be found in the *Kebra Nagast* or *Book of the Kings* (of Ethiopia). When Bayna Lehkem (son of King Solomon, whom he begot with the queen of Sheba, also known as Makeda) first visited Jerusalem, everybody who saw him—even King Solomon himself—was awestruck. Bayna, in their very own words, was "the perfect likeness of Solomon, the king" (*Kebra Nagast*, 41).

The people who served in the king's court could not distinguish Bayna from the king. They had just exited the chamber where King Solomon was still seated on his throne—only to meet him standing outside in the courtyard. They dashed inside, and lo and behold, he was seated on his throne! Again, they hurried outside, and he was still standing there, reasoning with one of his workmen. How could the king be in two places at the same time? After they realized Bayna was Solomon's son, they remarked that he was "fashioned perfectly in the likeness of his father's form and appearance" (*Kebra Nagast*, 47).

For King Solomon, Bayna was the epitome of King David, Solomon's father. As he embraced and pressed him against his bosom, he remarked, "David has renewed his youth, and has risen from the dead" (*Kebra Nagast*, 46). Bayna looked like David and Solomon in physical appearance, mannerisms, and cheerful disposition.

In the same way Bayna inherited distinct biological characteristics from his kinsman, so have we inherited spiritual and emotional elements of personality from our Creator. These godlike attributes enable us to fellowship with him. Right here, on earth, Jah established a perfect divine-human relationship with our first parents. Truly, they were the true archetype of humankind. They were the perfect godlike creature with whom he willed to share the newly created creation.

Jah gave our first parents full control "over the works of his hands" (Genesis 1:26, 28 KJV). He also advised them to subdue the earth and use its natural resources for their well-being and established a basic law:

> Of every tree in the garden thou mayest freely eat;
> but of the tree of the knowledge of good and evil,
> thou shalt not eat of it, for in the day that thou eatest
> thereof, thou shalt surely die. (Genesis 2:16–17 KJV)

As the true archetype of humankind, they had to be put to the test. They had to "prove" themselves and decide whether they were going to abide by what our Father had said to them.

Adam and Eve must have wondered why only the tree of the knowledge of good and evil was forbidden? Why was the acquisition of the knowledge of good and evil prohibited? Further, why was partaking of a tree that was pleasant to the sight—and good for food—a sin for which they were bound to die?

Obviously, that prohibition did not extend to the tree of life, which was also located in the middle of the garden. I believe it was the closest tree to the forbidden one. The forbidden tree was one that would cause humans to know good from bad, and the tree of life would have made them live forever.

Our first parents could have eaten freely from the tree of life without fear, but did they know that that tree that was growing right next to the forbidden tree could make them live forever?

> You may freely eat of every tree except the tree of the knowledge of good and evil. (Genesis 2:1–17 KJV)

When they disobeyed the command, they were expelled from the garden because Jah feared that they would "eat also from the tree of life and live forever" (Genesis 3:22–23 KJV). Evidently, it was a crucial moment of choice: to eat or not to eat, to obey the command or do the very opposite and face the consequences.

The tempter probably targeted Eve because she appeared to be more gullible and weak-willed. After a moment of resistance (telling the tempter what she was not supposed to do), she succumbed. The devil caused her to doubt and distrust the power and authority of Jahweh.

Jah said "Ye shall surely die" (Genesis 2:17 KJV), and the tempter said, "Ye shall not ... your eyes shall be opened, and ye shall be like God, Jah" (Genesis 3:4–5 KJV). Eve was supposed to trust Jah and take him at his word. Trust consists of not doubting. Instead, she—wanting to be like God—took the devil at his word.

The tempter made Eve believe that the forbidden tree was a must-have, a tree to be desired, one she could not live without. Not partaking was no longer an option for Eve:

> And when the woman saw ... that it was good ... a tree to be desired to make one wise, she took of the fruit ... and did eat and gave also unto her husband ... and he did eat. (Genesis 3:6 KJV)

Did the man know that the fruit his wife gave him to eat on the morning of the fall was from the forbidden tree? Was he with her when she took of the fruit? They both knew the tree of the knowledge of good and evil, and they would have also known its fruit. For this reason, I do believe that Adam could have refused to partake of the forbidden fruit, but—probably out of sympathy for his deceived wife—he chose to eat it.

The tempter knew that Adam was the image and glory of the Lord, Jah, and that his wife was the glory of the man. If he could deceive the woman, she could make the man do her bidding, which inevitably was that of the evil one.

Seemingly, Adam decided that he was going down with his wife. Could that be the reason lots of men today tell their female companions that they will do anything—anything—for them and that they cannot live without them?

Today, there is a lot of speculation and ongoing debate about what sin our first parents committed by partaking of a tree that was good for food. Some people even express doubt about whether the Garden of Eden even existed at all. And if it did, was it an actual fruit that they ate? Some hold that because we often refer to our off springs as the result or "fruits" of our copulation, Adam and Eve did not eat an actual fruit and had sexual intercourse instead. That suggestion seems a bit far-fetched to me since they were husband and wife together and were free to copulate. It was not a sin for them to have sex since they were free to be fruitful and multiply.

I believe that the garden of Eden existed, it was real, and there was nothing mythical about it. The Bible gave specific geographical references that can give us an idea about where Eden was located. I also believe that the fruit was a real edible fruit.

The scriptures gave us the names of four rivers that were associated with the garden of Eden (Genesis 2:11–14 KJV). The name of the third river is the Hiddekel. Hiddekel is the ancient name for the Tigris River. The fourth river is the Euphrates. These two rivers are in the Near East and they both join before emptying into the Persian Gulf. The Pishon and the Gihon are the names of the first and second rivers. Unfortunately, some biblical scholars hold that all attempts at identifying these two rivers as well as the land through which they flow are speculative and should remain tentative.

However, some scholars hold that the Pishon River could be either the Indus or the Ganges Rivers in India. They believe the Gihon must be the Nile because it encompasses the whole land of Cush (Ethiopia).

In the early nineteenth century, W. F. Albright was convinced that the Pishon and the Gihon were the Blue and the White Nile respectively. The Pishon or the Blue Nile flows out of the Ethiopian highlands, and the Gihon or the White Nile originates in Uganda. They both join to form the single, larger Nile that flows through Egypt. I am pleased to know that there are nonbiblical sources that also attested to the fact that the garden of Eden did exist. However, we choose to view this subject through the spectacle of the Bible as we know it today.

The Pishon and the Gihon cannot be the Blue and the White Nile, and I would not associate the Pishon with the Indus or the Ganges Rivers in India. The Pishon and the Gihon—as written in the scriptures—must be near the Euphrates and the Tigris Rivers since they are part of the "four heads" that formed after the river that watered Eden parted.

The Bible associated the Pishon River with the land of Havilah. In *From Babylon to Timbuktu* (15–16), Dr. Rudolph R. Winsor affirmed that the land of Havilah was widely known and that it was named after Havilah, a son of Cush, the Ethiopian (Genesis 10:7 KJV). That is the naked truth, and truth is not speculative. Therefore, the truth cannot be treated as tentative according to some scholars.

Clearly, the land was in the same Euphrates-Tigris plain where the Havilites or Ethiopians also dwelled. One must not forget that Ethiopia's ancient boundary once spanned across Arabia and Southern Asia as far as India. The *Kebra Nagast* contains Ethiopia's ancient boundaries (16, 163). In addition, in *From Babylon to Timbuktu*, Dr. Windsor said that there was a western as well as an eastern Ethiopian civilization in ancient times (14), which puts one of those ancient civilization in southern Mesopotamia.

It appears that Albright lacked knowledge of the ancient Ethiopian boundary. Further, he never knew that, when one talks about Ethiopia, he was also talking about the entire African continent (*From Babylon to Timbuktu*, 53). For Albright, Ethiopia was simply that mountainous country that occupies the northeastern part of African—and nowhere else.

The Pishon flows through the land of Havilah, which is the land of the Ethiopians, and the Gihon encompasses the whole land of Cush. Therefore, that puts both these rivers in the Euphrates-Tigris plain, which means that the well-watered garden of Eden must have also been there as well.

In any case, Eden should be taken to be the actual garden itself and not the larger landmass in which it was located. Also, the fruit was real, and it did not possess any unusual or mystical powers. Therefore, it would not have been the actual eating of the fruit that brought about the fall. It was disobedience; it was Adam and Eve's blatant rejection of Jahweh's authority, which led to their demise—and ultimately our demise.

Our God, Jah, purposed to teach our first parents very early in life that whenever they were faced with a crucial moment of choice, they had within themselves the power to obey or disobey, to choose to do what is right instead of what is wrong, and to discern what is good instead of bad. The choices they make will affect the quality of the life they live. Poor choices have severe consequences.

Unfortunately, our first parents transgressed. They disobeyed the prohibition, and disobedience is an act of rebellion against Jahweh. Accordingly, they acquired the knowledge of good and evil; they realized they had made the wrong choice when they chose against Jah, their Creator.

Instantly, the divine-human union that existed between Creator and creature was severed. Humans lost their godlikeness, and the living image of the living God was broken. For the first time, they realized that they were naked, and they felt vulnerable and helpless. They no longer felt worthy of being in the presence of Jahweh; they hid themselves, and the nagging thoughts of rapprochement engulfed them.

Jah expelled them both from Eden, and they lost it all. Spiritually, they became separated from their Creator, and physically, the easygoing, abundant life at its fullest became laborious and sorrowful. Also, the certainty of physical death became apparent. Outside Eden, the human way of life and state of the soul spiraled downward.

Deprived of godlikeness, humans quickly demonstrated that they were incapable of true fellowship—even with their own kind—and that manifested itself immediately after they began to reproduce. The senseless slaying of Abel at the hands of his very own brother magnifies man's fallen nature. Left to his own devices, he continued to degenerate. It got so bad that Jah, at one time, was sorry he had made man:

> God [Jah] saw ... that every imagination of the thoughts of his heart was only evil continually, and it repented the LORD [Jah] that he had made man on the earth. (Genesis 6:5–6 KJV)

As might be expected, man did attempt to reconcile himself to his Creator, but the broken image was incapable of mending itself. Man descended into the sin of idolatry. He so desperately wanted to reunite with his Creator that he created his own god. He probably believed that by having an idol that he can call god, he could reconnect with Jahweh, the true God. Man, in his fallen state thought that—like the tempter told Eve—he had become like his Creator. Therefore, he created his own idol (god) in his own image and likeness.

In his heart, man knew that his graven image was not his god since he was the maker of that lifeless image. Nevertheless, it was unlike the very character of Jahweh to sit back and watch the degeneration of his prized creation—the one he fashioned in his very own likeness and image. Compelled by love, he effected a plan of salvation to reconcile mankind to himself. The plan for salvation was a holistic plan that focused on man's spiritual as well as his physical, earthly needs. Interestingly, it also has a futuristic element to it.

Without any qualms, Haile Selassie I echoed that divine plan of salvation in his utterances. He shared the opinion that material well-being is of equal importance to spiritual and moral welfare. Unfortunately, most religious pundits today see salvation only in a purely spiritual, as well as an otherworldly or out-of-this-world sense.

Spiritually, the divine plan tackles original sin and its attendant consequences. Jahweh purposed to cleanse humanity from original sin and create clean hearts and right spirits. Eventually, the broken image of the living God, Jah, would be restored, and humanity would realize Edenic living—as it was before the fall—right here on earth. Ultimately, Jahweh's will would be done right here on this earth—just as it had been done in Zion.

Jahweh has chosen a rather bloody path to reconcile humanity by divine law:

> Almost all things are by the law purged with blood,
> and without shedding of blood is no remission.
> (Hebrews 9:22 KJV)

The first person to make a blood sacrifice for original sin after the fall was Abel. A blood sacrifice was a simple act of confession and repentance, but it never took away sin:

> For it is not possible that the blood of bulls and goats
> should take away sin. (Hebrews 10:4 KJV)

Through the practice of animal sacrifice, Jah implored man, firstly, to recognize his decayed spiritual status and then to entreat forgiveness. When performed with a contrite heart, Jah would pass over the sins of the offender.

In times past, to purge with blood on the national level, the high priest would perform a sacrifice once a year for himself and the populace. Jahweh's aim was to prepare humanity for the coming of a high priest who would be the sacrificial lamb whose blood alone would be the ultimate cure for original sin. When that high priest comes, his blood would cure original sin.

Like Haile Selassie, this writer finds glory in the Bible. It says that Eyesus Kristos (Jesus Christ) was that high priest, ordained by Jah, the Father, to make the one-time sacrifice for sin. He accomplished that mission on the cross more than two thousand years ago. Through his own blood, he obtained eternal redemption for fallen humanity. That means that we must no longer be concerned about original sin or the universal sinfulness of humanity. The cure for sin has already been applied—period.

We have all been freed from the clutches of original sin, but we are still free to shun or to commit personal sins, and we still die physically. The good news is that grace is the divine remedy for personal sin:

> For where sin abounded, grace did much more abound. (Romans 5:20 KJV)

Grace can be defined as the unmerited favor granted to us by Jahweh. Through the mechanism of the cross, he has sworn by his own right hand to pass over our sins.

The very second after Eyesus died on the cross, our sins were washed away—even though none of us here were alive then. We have all been saved from sin and its consequences. There is nothing we could have done to save ourselves. Jahweh did for us what we could not have done for ourselves, and for that, we must give him thanks and praise. As easy as that, we—the children of the Most High—have been saved from sin.

The scripture says that in the same way that Adam brought death upon humanity, even so did Eyesus—the second Adam—brought life to all. Yes, we all have passed from spiritual death to life, and that is the reason why we all still have some form of godlikeness. Nevertheless, we continue to die physically. Although death in this sense can be regarded as biological cessation, it can also be taken as being out from the body—and to be out of the body is to be present with Jahweh.

Right now, Jah alone is immortal. Humans are still mortal, but I believe that physical death was never a part of Jahweh's original plan for humanity. Although humans are full of spiritual and physical life, only the soul was immortal—the body is not. Had our first parents obeyed the command of Jahweh, at the proper time, their physical bodies also would have been immortalized, and they would have lived forever.

While every tree in the garden was good for food, there was one tree that was also good for immortality, and that is the tree of life. All our first parents were supposed to do was to eat from every other tree except the forbidden tree. That means that they would have automatically eaten from the tree of life.

Again, there was no prohibition on eating from the tree of life. The tree of life was standing there, just waiting to immortalize humankind. It displeased Jahweh greatly after Adam and Eve disobeyed the prohibition on eating from the tree of the knowledge of good and evil. Therefore, he expelled them speedily from the garden "lest they ... take of the tree of life, and eat, and live forever" (Genesis 3:22 KJV). That is part of the futuristic element of salvation that we, the children of the Most High, hope for.

When viewed in a purely spiritual sense, salvation has absolutely nothing to do with the afterlife or the pie-in-the-sky idea where people drink milk and honey and walk on streets paved with gold. Spiritual salvation embodies the reconciliation of humanity with the Creator—right here on earth—and that took effect immediately after what Eyesus did on the cross. His sacrificial death has broken sin's universal clasp around Jah's children.

Every adult is still responsible for their own personal, daily sin, and where sin is plentiful, the grace of Jahweh will be even more plentiful. Not one of us could have done anything to be saved; Jah has already saved us—period!

John, an apostle of Eyesus, spoke about the physical dimension of salvation:

> I wish above all things that you prosper and be in
> good health, even as thy soul prospereth. (3 John
> 1:2 KJV)

Even though most New Testament writers deemed salvation to be more of a spiritual issue, they seemingly never overlooked the earthly, physical concerns of humanity. That was quite evident in the early church at Jerusalem where the people shared their material possessions:

> Neither was there any among them that lacked ...
> distribution was made unto every man according as
> he had need. (Acts 4:34–35 KJV)

James, the doubtful brother of Eyesus, was leader of the early church at Jerusalem. Like Moses, he also taught devoted service for others. He encouraged his brethren in the faith to visit and show compassion for widows and the other unfortunate people in their community. James saw such service as more of an earthly dimension to divine compassion. He believed that one should live clean and let their works be seen.

Recent history also showed that the beloved Marcus Garvey shared similar sentiments. To him, spiritual and socioeconomic well-being are interlaced. He promoted the concept of socioeconomic salvation for the people who descended from those who Moses brought out of Egyptian bondage and survived slavery in the New World. He taught during the time when the people of African descent were being looked upon as the outcast of the races and the laughingstock of civilization.

For hundreds of years before the coming of Marcus Garvey, we were told that salvation was a deeply spiritual and thoroughly otherworldly matter—a matter only for the soul. We were told that it was all right to live in poverty here on the earth because when you die you will go up to heaven and be rich. The preachers misconstrued the scripture that says "the love of money is the root of all evil" (1 Timothy 6:10 KJV).

As might be expected, many people believed that to even have their basic wants and needs—food, clothes, and shelter—met was vain and sinful. And sin's reward, in those days, was hellfire. Therefore, the people sang, "You can take the whole world—but give me Jesus."

Time after time, the ignorant preachers would remind churchgoers that they cannot take their money or material possessions to heaven when they die. Therefore, they took very little interest in accumulating wealth. They settled below the poverty line.

That pie-in-the-sky concept of salvation that many so-called Christians still advocate today is slavish foolery and should be renounced and denounced immediately. Marcus Garvey taught that it is better to be honestly wealthy than to be miserably poor. He tied together the spiritual and the physical dimensions of salvation. As much as we all would like to go to heaven, we must remember that we are living on earth. Right now, we are living on earth; therefore, we must first pay attention to our basic, earthly wants and needs. That is the beatitude of bread and butter. Again, socioeconomic salvation is the salvation we all hope for in the West.

Let it be known that they can fool some people sometimes, but they can't fool all the people all the time. Salvation should be taken to mean deliverance from sickness, natural disaster, poverty, political and religious persecution, personal enemies, and even the accomplishment of personal dreams and aspirations. Salvation, in its totality, embodies deliverance from any dreadful situation from which one is unable to rid oneself. One can then proceed to lead a quiet and peaceable life in their community.

The writers of the Old Testament seemed to have had a better overstanding of salvation than those of the so-called New Testament. According to *The Anchor Bible Dictionary* (908–909), salvation was "very earthly" since "divine and human action" seem to go hand in glove. That is the earthly dimension to divine deliverance.

One of the most intriguing Bible stories that echoes the earthly dimension to divine deliverance is the Exodus from Egypt. Moses was nothing more than the human agent raised up by Jahweh to save his people from Egyptian slavery and to give them political autonomy and prosperity in Canaan. Ultimately, Jahweh delivered the people at the Sea of Reeds. As it were, Moses was the glove, and Jah was the hand in the glove.

Moses tried to console the people who were afraid of the pursuing Egyptian army:

> Fear not, stand still, and see the salvation of the LORD [Jah] which he will show to you. (Exodus 14:13 KJV)

Moses did his part, and Jah saved Israel from the Egyptians. That token of earthly salvation had profound spiritual implications. After the people realized what Jahweh had just done for them, they sang songs and danced to his honor and glory:

> The people feared the LORD [Jah] and believed on him and his servant Moses. (Exodus 14:31 KJV)

When we talk about the future element of salvation, we are also talking about the time of final restoration. It is the time appointed by the Father—when all twelve tribes of Israel shall be reunited and shall follow the house of David. Jahweh shall come and shall restore the kingdom of Judah, right here on earth:

> Israel did rebel against the House of David ... and
> there was none that followed the house of David but
> the tribe of Judah only. (1 Kings 12:19–20 KJV)

Meanwhile, the chastisement continued, and the house of David continued to suffer violence because the violent had taken it by force.

Jah warned our ancestors that he would not fail to punish them if they did not choose to observe to do all his commands and his statutes. They shall be scattered among all people, from one end of the earth to the other.

Moses said that one of the methods of worldwide dispersion would be by ship:

> Jah shall bring them into Egypt (bondage) again
> with ships ... and there they would be sold unto their
> enemies for male and female slaves. (Deuteronomy
> 28:64, 68. KJV)

Those prophetic words were fulfilled during the transatlantic slave trade. Tens of millions of black Hebrew-Israelites were taken from the kingdom of Judah in Africa, forced across the Atlantic Ocean to the so-called New World, and sold as slaves. After dehumanizing and using us for hundreds of years, they turned and lynched us, scorned us, and refused us. Yes, they made the same mistake that our enemies made in the past:

> They have taken crafty counsel against Jah People
> and consulted against his hidden ones. They have
> said, come, and let us cut them off from being a
> nation; that the name of Israel may be no more in
> remembrance. (Psalm 83:3—4 KJV)

Today, we take comfort in the prophetic words of our God, Jah, which Isaiah penned for us:

> O Israel, thou shall not be forgotten by me … I have
> blotted out, like a thick cloud, thy transgressions,
> and, like a cloud, thy sins; return unto me for I have
> redeemed thee. (Isaiah 44:21–22 KJV)

Our God, Jah, made a promise to us and Jeremiah prophesied:

> Fear not; for I am with thee. I will bring thy seed
> from the east and gather thee from the west. I will
> say to the North, Give up; and to the south, Keep
> not back; bring my sons from far, and my daughters
> from the ends of the earth. Everyone who is called
> by my name; for I have created him for my glory.
> (Isaiah 43:5–7 KJV)

> The days come when we shall say, "The LORD [Jah]
> liveth, who brought up and who led the seed of the
> house of Israel out of the north country, and from
> all countries to which I had driven them, and they
> shall dwell in their own land." (Jeremiah 23:8 KJV)

The coming House, or kingdom of David, is a literal, earthly kingdom over which that righteous branch of David shall rule. In fact, it will be the kingdom of Jah right here on this very earth. That is what Eyesus was looking forward to when he taught his apostles to say, "Thy kingdom come [on earth] and thy will be done on earth" (Luke 11:2 KJV).

The biblical Ethiopia with its original biblical boundary markings is the continent from which he shall govern the earth. It is a self-sufficient continent. With its known, vast amounts of natural resources, fine climate, and arable lands, Ethiopia shall see the return of Edenic conditions when the appointed time comes:

The desert shall rejoice, and blossom like the rose.
(Isaiah 35:1 KJV)

The land flows with milk and honey. It's laden with gold, silver, diamonds, copper, iron, coal, platinum, oil, salt, water, and other minerals. Truly, Ethiopia shall become the earthly paradise.

Jahweh has promised the return of the righteous branch of David, who shall reign, prosper, and execute justice and judgment in the earth. Our communities shall be free from agitation, and political upheavals will be unheard of. Under the leadership of the Conquering Lion of the tribe of Judah, all nations shall "beat their swords into plowshares, and their spears into pruning hooks … neither shall they learn war anymore" (Isaiah 2:4 KJV).

As a token of salvation, Jeremiah said, "It is good that a man should both hope and quietly wait for the salvation of the LORD [Jah]" (Lamentations 3:26 KJV). Selah.

Chapter 5

The Ten Commandments

EYESUS KRISTOS (JESUS Christ) once told an expert in Jewish law that all the law and prophets were based upon two commandments only.

> There is no other commandment greater than these.
> (Mark 12:31 KJV)

> Hear, O Israel: The LORD our God is one LORD: And thou shalt love the LORD thy God with all thine heart ... with all thy soul ... with all thy might. (Deuteronomy 6:4–5 KJV)

> Thou shalt love thy neighbor as thyself. (Leviticus 19:18 KJV)

There are hundreds of commandments, and of the hundreds, our God has singled out another ten that he wanted us, the children of Israel, to pay particular attention to.

In the two commandments mentioned above, the title LORD appears three times. Also, it is written in all uppercase letters. As a reminder, the title Lord was intentionally written with all capital letters to show us exactly where the name of our God, Jah, was written in the original ancient text before it was removed and replaced with the title Lord.

When that portion of scripture was drafted into the New Testament, not one of King James's fifty-four independent scholars—who he hired to translate the Bible out of the original tongues—seemed to have cared about retaining the name Jah wherever they encountered it in the original documents. There is only place in the entire King James Version of the Bible where they kept the proper name of our God in place:

> Sing praises to his name: extol him that rideth upon
> the heavens by his name Jah, and rejoice before him.
> (Psalm 68:4)

They knew that the proper name of our God is Jah, but they decided that they were going to let it remain in that psalm as evidence.

Our God, Jah, singled out the Ten Commandments (Deuteronomy 5:6–21 KJV):

I.   I am Jah thy God, who brought thee out of the land of Egypt, from the house of bondage. Thou shall have no other gods before me.

II. Thou shall not make unto thee any graven image, or any likeness of anything that is in heaven above, or that is in the earth beneath, or that is in the water under the earth. Thou shall not bow down thyself to them, nor serve them; for I, Jah thy God, am a jealous God, visiting the iniquity of the fathers upon the children unto the third and fourth generation of them that hate me; and showing mercy unto thousands of them that love me, and keep my commandments.

III. Thou shall not take the name of Jah, thy God in vain; for I, Jah, will not hold him guiltless that taketh my name in vain.

IV.   Remember the sabbath day, to keep it holy, as Jah thy God hath commanded thee. Six days shall you labor and do all thy work. But the seventh day is the sabbath of Jah thy God; in it you shall not do any work, you, nor your son, nor your daughter, your manservant, nor your maidservant, nor your cattle, nor any stranger that is within thy gates; that thy manservant and thy maidservant may rest as well as thou. And remember that thou was a servant in the land of Egypt, and that Jah thy God brought thee out from there through a mighty hand and by an outstretched arm; therefore, I, Jah, thy God commanded thee to keep the sabbath day.

V.   Honor thy father and thy mother, as Jah thy God hath commanded thee, that thy days may be long, and that it may go well with thee in the land which Jah thy God giveth thee.

VI.   Thou shall not kill.

VII.   Thou shall not commit adultery.

VIII.   Thou shall not steal.

IX.   Thou shall not bear false witness against thy neighbor.

X.   Thou shall not covet thy neighbor's house; thou shall not covet thy neighbor's wife, nor his manservant, nor his maidservant, nor his ox, nor his ass, nor anything that is thy neighbor's.

The sacred name, Jah, occurred ten times in the Ten Commandments, and it is my belief that Moses uttered the name aloud so that the children of Israel could hear it.

In the third commandment, Jah cautioned us not to take his name in vain. He also made it abundantly clear that we would be held accountable for doing so. Nevertheless, what is most heartening to me is that he did not forbid us from calling upon his name; he did not impose a prohibition on the uttering of his name, as some learned clergymen want us to believe. In addition, it comforts me to know that it is not an unforgivable sin by scriptural standards if we were to fail to follow that command.

He warned that there should never be any vainglory or vain display whenever we utter his name. Whenever we utter that sacred name, we should do so in a manner that brings glory to the name. We should never utter his name simply because we know it. One must not forget that our Father's name is holy and should express reverence whenever we utter that name.

Our Father wants us, his Hebrew-Israelite sons and daughters who are still suffering here in the West, to call upon his name:

> Whosoever shall call upon the name, Jah, shall be delivered. (Joel 2:32 KJV)

> Moses and Aaron among his priests, and Samuel among those who call upon his name; they called upon the name, Jah, and he answered them. (Psalm 99:6 KJV)

I think it would be expedient here to remind us all that humans began to openly call upon the name Jah after Seth—the one appointed by our God to replace Abel whom Cain murdered—had his own son. After Seth found out that he had been sent to replace Abel, he named his very own son, Enoch, which means "mortal." Clearly, Seth understood that—like his brother Abel—he and his son were also mortal beings, still awaiting immortality (Genesis 4:26 KJV).

I will conclude with a psalm from the New Scofield Reference Bible, and I will insert the name Jah wherever he did write it in the ancient manuscript. In this particular psalm, he was giving thanks and praise to his God, our God, for his faithfulness to those who trust in him:

OH give thanks unto Jah; call upon his name ...
Glory ye in his holy name; let the heart of them
rejoice who seek Jah. Seek Jah, and his strength; seek
his face evermore. (Psalm 105:1–4)

Selah.

9 781489 7323